Praise for *Compelling Conversations for Fundraisers*

"**To make the ask, you need this book, whether you're a new fundraiser or an old hand.** *Compelling Conversations for Fundraisers* provided me, a development professional with 20+ years experience, many fresh ways to approach donors and effectively make the ask."

Liz Leshin, Director of Development
LOS ANGELES CONSERVANCY

"*Compelling Conversations for Fundraisers* reminds us that **human interests drive philanthropy** and encourages fundraisers to weave authenticity through their conversations."

Natalie Rodriguez Jansorn, Director, College Excellence Program
THE ASPEN INSTITUTE

"Janet and Laurie **take the mystery out of asking for money** by breaking conversations down to a very easy-to-understand and applicable level."

Gregory Bradbard, President & CEO
INLAND EMPIRE UNITED WAY

"*Compelling Conversations for Fundraisers* **helps us to bring donors and prospects closer to our organization** and to their own philanthropic dreams."

Lisa Van Ingen Pope, Senior VP of Branch Financial Development
YMCA OF METROPOLITAN LOS ANGELES

"*Compelling Conversations for Fundraisers* brings keen focus, and **helps take the 'rush' out of preparing for key pitch meetings** so I'm able to go in grounded, confident, and ready to listen."

Sue Schardt, Executive Director
AIRMEDIA.ORG

"A **refreshing and a profound tool** that reminds us skills such as listening, being direct and simply having a conversation about our shared passions touches our basic need to be heard and make the connection with other like-minded people."

Debbie A. Cannon
ACADEMY FOR GRASSROOTS ORGANIZATIONS

Compelling Conversations for Fundraisers:
Talk Your Way to Success with Donors and Funders

Janet Levine
Laurie A. Selik

CHIMAYO PRESS

Los Angeles
2016

Compelling Conversations for Fundraisers:
Talk Your Way to Success with Donors and Funders

© Copyright Janet Levine and Laurie A. Selik

Levine, Janet, 1947- author.
Compelling conversations for fundraisers : talk your
way to success with donors and funders / Janet Levine,
Laurie A. Selik.
pages cm
Includes bibliographical references.
LCCN 2015951420
ISBN 978-0-9904988-0-3
ISBN 978-0-9904988-1-0 (e-book)

1. Nonprofit organizations--Finance. 2. Fundraising.
3. Interpersonal communication. I. Selik,
Laurie A., author. II. Title.

HG4027.65.L475 2015   658.1
                           6QBI15-600220

Chimayo Press
3766 Redwood Avenue
Los Angeles, CA 90066 USA
ChimayoPress.com
Telephone: 01- (310) 390-0131

Compelling Conversations for Fundraisers:
Talk Your Way to Success with Donors and Funders

© Copyright Janet Levine and Laurie A. Selik

Levine, Janet, 1947- author.
Compelling conversations for fundraisers : talk your
way to success with donors and funders / Janet Levine,
Laurie A. Selik.
pages cm
Includes bibliographical references.
LCCN 2015951420
ISBN 978-0-9904988-0-3
ISBN 978-0-9904988-1-0 (e-book)

1. Nonprofit organizations--Finance. 2. Fundraising.
3. Interpersonal communication. I. Selik,
Laurie A., author. II. Title.

HG4027.65.L475 2015   658.1
6QBI15-600220

Chimayo Press
3766 Redwood Avenue
Los Angeles, CA 90066 USA
ChimayoPress.com
Telephone: 01- (310) 390-0131

Dedicated to all donors and fundraisers who believe in holding compelling conversations and make change possible.

TABLE OF CONTENTS

Introduction 1

Chapter 1: Values and the Case Statement 3

Chapter 2: Acquiring New Donors..21

Chapter 3: Renewing Donors 37

Chapter 4: Re-Engaging Donors...49

Chapter 5: Upgrading Donors 61

Chapter 6: Planned Gifts, Endowments and Bequests 71

Chapter 7: The Integrated Ask...87

Chapter 8: Foundations and Conversations 95

Resources 105

About the Authors 123

About Chimayo Press 125

INTRODUCTION

Today, the pressure is on to meet our fundraising goals. We focus on database lists, moves management and galas. At times we may forget one of the reasons we were drawn to a fundraising career in the first place—the opportunity to develop quality relationships with like-minded, generous people who also support worthy causes. We may fail to make time to hold real conversations with donors, perhaps the essential building block in sustaining their interest in your organization and sustaining your stamina in this field.

Compelling Conversations for Fundraisers gives you the tools to really learn about your donors through personal interaction and includes conversation guides to:

• Turn a social conversation to one about the mission of your group.

• Refresh and deepen your conversations with donors.

• Create a more positive fundraising experience for your donors and establish a more satisfying work experience for you as a fundraiser.

When you choose to prepare for compelling conversations with your donors, the result will be more thoughtful interaction that will provide context for you—the listener and relationship-builder—to ask follow-up questions, to relate to your donor's answer and to truly interact with the person in front of you. Whether you are working in the advancement department of a large university or a one-person development office for a small non-profit, we think you'll find by creating real conversations, your donors will feel heard and appreciated. At the same time, your organization will build a list of loyal donors who contribute and feel part of your community.

Compelling Conversations for Fundraisers' eight chapters include advice, examples of compelling conversations and conversation starters for each stage in donor cultivation: Acquiring New Donors, Re-Engaging Donors, Renewing Donors and Upgrading Donors. We encourage you to role play with your colleagues, or classmates, and on your own using the many conversation starters provided in this workbook style text.

Are you working on planned gifts? We also include a chapter on this important area that may yield your largest contributions. Foundation program officers are people too—so we've included a chapter on how you can get to know them better and build relationships to benefit your organization.

We hope you find in these pages the sparks for a new approach and the confidence to truly engage your donors. After all, isn't a good conversation one of life's great pleasures?

Janet Levine and Laurie A. Selik

CHAPTER 1
VALUES AND THE CASE STATEMENT

Who are you?

That's not just a rhetorical question. Before you can have compelling conversations with your donors, it's important that you have clarity about and understanding of your organization. You need to know not just what your mission is, or what programs you have, but also what you accomplish—why your organization makes a difference. In this chapter we introduce how you can use values to have deeper conversations with your donors.

If your organization writes grants or has recently led a specific fundraising campaign, you probably have some sort of case statement. While a case statement often ends up as a case for giving—(usually) a glossy sales brochure—we are focusing on your internal case statement: the document from which you build all your fundraising materials.

Above all, the case statement answers our very first question: *Who are you?*

Nonprofits are mission driven organizations, so your case starts, appropriately enough, with your mission. Notice that we did not say "mission statement," though if your mission statement clarifies why your organization exists, use it. If it does not, or does so imperfectly, craft a few sentences that explain the purpose of your organization.

➡ What is your mission? . . . .
. . . .
. . . .
. . . .
. . . .
. . . .

Your leadership's vision for what lies ahead is also important. If your organization has a current strategic plan, you may have worked on vision statements. However, not all organizations actually have a vision. Janet worked at a community college where the president railed at the idea of vision. "Vision," he would steam, "we have no vision. We're a community college."

While that was disheartening, his perspective also brought to the forefront an important issue for the institution. As the immortal Yogi Berra is credited with saying, "If you don't know where you are going, you might wind up someplace else."

"Someplace else" is probably not where you want your organization to go. But where do you want to go? That is the question your vision answers.

If your leadership has created a vision for your organization, write it down in the space below. If there isn't a current vision, consider what you think the direction of your organization ought to be. Then write your vision of what your organization aims to be or do in the future, not just your purpose today.

➲ What is your vision? Where is your organization headed? (Think big and be specific). . . . .
. . . .
. . . .
. . . .
. . . .
. . . .

Standard case statements go from mission and vision to answering a series of specific questions that discuss your organization's history, challenges faced, and solutions to those challenges—including financial solutions. We provide a complete description on what a compelling case statement covers in the Resources section.

WHY VALUES MATTER

For our purposes, developing the case for having compelling fundraising conversations shines a spotlight on one critical area: values. Our favorite definition of values is "the importance, worth, or usefulness of something."

Values are the things that have meaning to your donors. They are the reasons they are motivated to support your organization. They range from Accomplishment to Zeal and tons of values in-between.

One of the trainings we do is called "Values Based Fundraising." We use the "Motivational Values" cards from a non-profit consulting practice called 21/64 (2164.net).

21/64 created the cards to help the next generation of donors consider how each of the 25 values described in the deck influences personal and/or philanthropic decisions. We use the cards to help those responsible for

VALUES LIST

Achievement
Balance
Community
Creativity
Democratic
Diversity
Excellence
Family-oriented
Growth
Joy
Positivity
Rigor
Service
Teamwork

See the Resources section for more.

fundraising (staff and volunteers) have meaningful conversations about giving. We believe, along with 21/64, that the more your decisions are aligned with your values, the more fulfilling and strategic they will be.

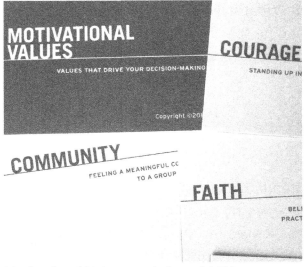

Motivational Values cards from 21/64.net.

➲ What values speak to you? Undoubtedly there are many. Among our top 10 are community, freedom, and opportunity. What are your top three values?

1. . . . .
2. . . . .
3. . . . .

In our trainings, we ask people to first chose a value card that calls to them today and then pair off into groups of two. The first part of the exercise is to simply tell the other person about the value chosen and why it matters to them. People tell us that these conversations are among the best they have ever had. They learn things about others they never would have uncovered. More importantly, they learn a lot about themselves.

The next exercise is to stay with your chosen partner and talk about your nonprofit based on the other person's value.

In real life, however, you don't have value cards that jump-start a conversation, and you may not know what the other person's values are. But if you approach a conversation about your organization from a values standpoint, you will soon find out.

Laurie, for example, works at a school that has a program providing underserved students a top notch performing arts education at no cost. She talks to her prospects and donors about the many programs her organization offers—how many classes, the teaching techniques, profiles of the students, accomplishments of the faculty. But to get someone's initial interest, she knows that most people don't care about how you go about what you do—they only care about what it means and how it changes lives. So Laurie approaches her prospects from a values point of view: for example, opportunity, education, excellence.

What I love most about the Colburn School is how we provide our students with opportunities they may not otherwise have to study music with world-class teachers. I'd love to have you visit us. It's so amazing to listen to our students as their teachers guide them to reach deep within themselves to play better than they did the day before. I see how students grow along with their commitment to music. And I have to tell you, it is magic. Do you think you have time for a tour sometime in the next two weeks?

By talking with her prospects and donors from a values standpoint, she avoids a common pitfall of losing her prospect before they get started because the first program she describes may not be one that has meaning to that prospect. With a values perspective, however, we are talking about something larger than seven-year-olds learning how to play violin.

When Janet does public trainings, she often asks people to introduce themselves, telling the rest of the group what their organization does. Inevitably, people talk about the programs the organizations offer, how old it is, its locations, the people it serves (usually "underserved populations") and afterward the group hasn't learned anything compelling about the organization.

"Here are the values that I stand for: honesty, equality, kindness, compassion, treating people the way you want to be treated and helping those in need. To me, those are traditional values."
—Ellen DeGeneres

Values are not history or activities. They represent the difference that your organization makes. Instead of saying, "We are a food bank that picks up food from local food stores and restaurants and has pantries in eight locations around our city. Our volunteer drivers pick up and deliver the food on a same-day basis, ensuring our clients get fresh food," consider what all this activity means.

We could use the value of compassion to talk about this organization, or one we mentioned above, community. We might talk about the fact that one in five children in the United States goes hungry every day. For example: "We work as a community of volunteers, food stores, restaurants, to ensure that those children get fresh food and can enjoy a hunger-free life."

➲ How might you tell a new acquaintance (or an old friend!) about your organization? Note that by using values, you are making these conversations personal. . . . .
. . . .
. . . .
. . . .
. . . .
. . . .
. . . .
. . . .
. . . .
. . . .
. . . .

So how does Laurie make her conversation about her organization—using one of the values we mentioned—opportunity—her own?

Laurie: *I was really lucky when I was growing up. My parents exposed me to so many cultural things—we read, listened to music, went to the theater. I really loved to tap dance and took lessons for years. It really opened the world up to me, and showed me so many possibilities. What I love about my organization is that, beyond music, it teaches kids who wouldn't otherwise have the opportunity the joy of learning.*

At this point, she stays quiet, and waits for the other person to respond. While she could also end that statement with a question, she would want to ensure that it is open-ended and not one that requires a simple yes or no.

How might you use a value to begin a conversation about the following types of organizations?

➲ Social services for developmentally disabled children: . . . .
. . . .
. . . .
. . . .
. . . .
. . . .
. . . .

➲ School (either K-12 or post-secondary): . . . .
. . . .
. . . .
. . . .
. . . .
. . . .
. . . .

➲ An environmental organization: . . . .
. . . .
. . . .
. . . .
. . . .
. . . .

➡ Your organization: . . . .
. . . .
. . . .
. . . .
. . . .
. . . .
. . . .
. . . .

You'll find that learning your donors' values through conversations will help you to make the all-important connection for them to your organization. They may know why they show up for performances or volunteer to deliver meals, but it's up to you to remind them of how your organization is delivering on their deeply held values and beliefs. If you can do that, you are likely to have a loyal donor.

A VALUES-BASED COMPELLING CONVERSATION

Bethany is the director of development of an organization that mentors low-income girls through writing. Amy, a board member, has invited her friend Kathie, a writer, to lunch. Long term, Amy and Bethany hope that Kathie will become a significant donor. Short term goal, however, is to get Kathie interested and willing to come and share her experiences as a young writer (decades ago!) with some of the girls. Now, the three women are seated at a table in Amy's favorite restaurant.

Kathie: *You've told me so much about this place, Amy—I'm so excited to finally get to eat here!*

Amy: *And I'm so excited to be able to get you together with Bethany and, I hope, our fabulous organization.*

Kathie smiles, but doesn't say anything. After a short silence, Bethany jumps in.

Bethany: *Kathie, what—if anything—do you know about our organization?*

Kathie: *Well, Amy keeps trying to get me to do either a panel or teach a workshop, so I know that. And I know that this is for young girls. But, really, that's all I know.*

Bethany: *That's a good start. And yes, we do produce panel discussions and workshops, but mainly we help girls have a voice.*

Kathie nods, but remains silent.

Bethany: *Most of our girls come from very low-income families. And, unfortunately, that usually means parents—or mainly parent, singular—have little education. These kids are smart, Kathie, but they don't know how to communicate, to articulate what they want, hope for, dream about. And that's what we offer.*

Kathie: *The girls are how old?*

Amy: *12 to 18. We work with the middle and high schools in our community to identify the best candidates.*

Kathie: *And what makes a girl a good candidate? Good behavior? Grades?*

Bethany shakes her head.

Bethany: *Not completely. We do get the good students but we also get the ones who are acting out and seem headed for trouble.*

Kathie: *That would have been me.*

She lowers her head and a small smile plays around her mouth.

Kathie: *I wanted so much when I was a kid—but I couldn't see how to get what I wanted.*

Amy: *That's why our organization is so important! We help these girls see a path and be able to talk about what they want. It makes them feel...*

Kathie: *Worthwhile?*

Amy: *Yes! And we have incredible results.*

They talk for awhile, telling Kathie about how the program keeps girls in schools and out of gangs. How many of their girls go on to college. Bethany pulls a book out of her briefcase.

Bethany: *And this is the book that we published last year. It's full of stories and poems by our girls. Another anthology will be coming out in another year. And now, one of our mentors is a playwright, and she is working with a group of girls to turn this story—she opens the book and points to a story—into a one act play. The girls hope to perform it at the Fringe Festival in Scotland next year.*

Kathie: *Wow! That's impressive. But honestly—are any of the difficult girls involved or is it all of the good students?*

Bethany: *We don't differentiate our girls by behavior or grades. We expect all to participate. That's the point. By finding their voices they all—every single one of them—realize what winners they are. That makes all of us stronger. So what do you say, Kathie—are you on board? Will you come and talk with our girls about how you broke into professional writing?*

Kathie: *Sign me up!*

THE PIVOT

One of the hardest parts of fundraising is moving your conversation to the topic of making a gift. Even if you are engaged in a conversation about values—and how your involvement with your organization helps you to live your values—it can feel daunting to lead the conversation to something a bit more specific. Turning the conversation from just social to having a compelling conversation about support for the organization takes finesse and practice.

We call this "the pivot" and you use it when you want to move the conversation to your purpose: whether learning your donors values or, when ready, to ask for a gift for your organization. The good news is that, handled correctly, it is no big deal. The secret is that you always remain clear about your intentions for the conversation or meeting.

For example, you met Susie at a chamber event. When you mentioned your organization, she told you that she was really interested in your cause. Naturally, you thought, "What a great prospect!"

So you decide to follow up. When you contact Susie to set up a time for the two of you to get together, the conversation (and note, this conversation can be on the phone, via email or even text) should *not* be:

Hi Susie, I so enjoyed meeting you and would love for us to get to know each other better. Can you do lunch on Thursday?

That may get you a lunch date, but Susie will undoubtedly be thinking the conversation will be mostly social. Instead, be very clear:

Hi Susie, I so enjoyed meeting you at the chamber mixer and hearing about your interest in (your cause/constituency/organization). *I would love for us to get together so I could tell you more and learn how you might become involved with us.*

She may very well say "No thanks. I was just blowing smoke and honestly, could care less about developmentally disabled dogs," but then you won't be wasting time with someone who we call affectionately a "China Egg" (i.e. will never hatch).

Pivoting, of course, is not only necessary when you make the appointment. It is a critical step when you are in the meeting. When Janet first started her fundraising career, she was Director of Corporate Relations at the University of Southern California's Viterbi School of Engineering. Much of her work was with senior corporate executives who partnered with her to get seriously large gifts for the school from their companies. At some point, Janet had a brainstorm: These are all high level, well paid guys (and back in the 1980's, they were all guys). I should talk to them about their personal gifts to the School.

Early in this process, one of her corporate contacts died. At the funeral, the gentleman's wife asked Janet to "give me a few months, then let's get together." Clearly her interest was in doing something in honor of her late husband.

A few months later, Janet called the wife and they arranged to have lunch. As they sat down, Janet asked how the wife was doing and was told that she was remodeling the house. They talked about that remodel until lunch was almost done and they were having coffee. Finally, the wife put her cup down and, looking straight at Janet, said, "You don't do this a lot do you?"

ALL EARS

Listen.

Let's face it, the most compelling conversations are the ones where you are at the center. But if you want to cultivate and ultimately solicit a prospect, your job is to let them shine.

She then went on to explain that she had lots of friends to talk with about her remodel. Lovely as Janet was, she wasn't this woman's friend. This lunch was to be about a gift in honor of the husband, and Janet's job was to turn—pivot—the conversation quickly to that point.

Humbling as it was, it was lesson that Janet never forgot.

FOCUSING ON YOUR GOAL

When your intention is to talk about a gift for your organization—whether it is a first or a fifty-first conversation—it is your job to keep focused on your goal and to watch the clock to be sure you save time to ask.

"Hi, Susie. Thanks so much for meeting with me. How is everything?" is a fine start. But let it be the start and once she says "everything is good," move right into your purpose for getting together.

Because this is a book about conversations, we want to be clear that at this point you do not launch into a monologue about the organization or the specific project for which you are raising funds. Rather, use this time to learn as much about your prospect and her potential interest as she will learn about you and/or the project.

How do you do that? By framing as much as you can as open-ended questions.

As I mentioned on the phone (in my email/text), I was really excited about your interest in the work that we do. How did you first get interested in...?

Then *listen* to what Susie says.

A SHORT BUT COMPELLING CONVERSATION—WITH A PIVOT

Richard is a top prospect at your organization. Charlene, the development director has tried—and failed—to get an appointment to move Richard from prospect to donor. She knows that her board member Joan and Joan's husband are friends of Richard so she is meeting with Joan to ask for her help in moving Richard.

Charlene: *Thanks for meeting with me, Joan. I know how busy you are.*

Joan: *It's just been crazy. You know our granddaughter is turning 16—and omigod, the preparations for her sweet sixteen. You'd think it was a wedding. I have spent I don't know how many hours helping my daughter decide on the place...*

Joan is off, talking-talking-talking and avoiding the topic at hand. Charlene must turn the conversation around. Finally, Joan takes a breath.

Charlene: *That sounds pretty intense. Your daughter is lucky that you are so willing to help—and I'm hoping that our organization will also be able to benefit from your assistance.*

Though she really doesn't want to give Joan a chance to change the subject back to her granddaughter's party, she knows she must be silent and let Joan respond. Which she does.

Joan: *Of course. I love this organization. That's why I serve on the board and have been so involved for so many years*

Charlene: *And we do appreciate your many contributions. Today I wanted to talk very specifically about Richard Taunton.*

Joan nods and says that he is an old friend.

Charlene: *That's why I am asking for your help. I've been trying to get a meeting with him for months, but I can't even get him on the phone. Can you help brainstorm some ideas? And to be honest, I'm hoping that you will join us in a meeting with me and Richard.*

GETTING A FIRST APPOINTMENT

Joe and Shirley have been on your radar for a while. They are known to be philanthropic, but you've been unable to find anyone within your organization who knows them, and you really have no reason to think they have a particular interest in your organization.

However, they came to your gala this year because they are the friend of a friend of the honoree. You meet them at the event and Joe gave you his business card. How might you first approach Joe? Remember to be clear about your purpose—not just to have a meeting but what the meeting will be about?

➲ Opening statement connecting Joe to your organization: . . . .
. . . .
. . . .
. . . .

. . . .

. . . .

. . . .

. . . .

. . . .

. . . .

. . . .

What will you say if Joe demurs? For example, you call Joe and after reminding him who you are you say, "I would really like to get together with you (and Shirley, if you think that best), and give you more information about our organization. Could we meet for coffee/lunch/ whatever *or* could I come to your office/house either Wednesday in the morning or Friday later in the afternoon?

In an ideal world, of course, Joe would say great. But in real life, Joe very well may say:

1. *No thanks. I'm just not interested.*

2. *I'm really busy now. It wouldn't be a good time.*

3. *If you are going to ask for a gift, I'm going to have to disappoint you.*

◉ What would your response be to each of those scenarios?

1. . . . .
2. . . . .
3. . . . .

Our recommendation, regardless of which excuse Joe gives you, is to first give it that old college try:

• *I understand. Is there an organization you are involved with currently?* (You might as well get information that you might be able to use if not now, then at a later date.)

Your pivot is a bridge from the current topic to the focused topic you want to discuss. Listen for natural pauses in the conversation and, with care, pivot to the point of your meeting. Your shift in the conversation may be indirect, as long as you know where you want to lead your donor.

Sample Pivot Phrases:

...I'm glad you brought that up, because [our organization] also...

...I'm hearing that you are concerned about what you will leave for your grandchildren. Did you know there are tax benefits for them with some planned gift products?

...Before it's time to go, I would like to share with you/ask you...

- *I understand. When would be a good time for me to reach out to you again?* (Building relationships takes time; just make sure that if he says, "after Christmas" you note it in your calendar and if he says, "After the big board meeting," you find out when that meeting is, and actually reach out to him again.)

- *To be honest, Joe, at some point I hope you will make a gift to organization. But we are a long way away from that point. As I said, I really would like to share with you the amazing work we do. Would you be able to meet for coffee next Wednesday at, say 9:30?* (Offering Joe a specific time focuses his response on when rather than whether.)

MEET, GREET...PIVOT!

Let's assume that Joe does, eventually, agree to meet. Plan how you will pivot the conversation after you've greeted Joe (and, perhaps, Shirley). Pretend you are a screenwriter and continue the script we've begun:

You: *Thank you so much for meeting with me. It's been awhile since we saw each other at the gala. How is everything?*

Joe: *As I mentioned on the phone, it's been a busy time. I had a big board meeting to prepare for.*

Shirley: *And just before then, our daughter Katie got engaged.*

You: *Congratulations! When is the wedding?*

Shirley tells you in six months, and proceeds to talk and talk about her daughter, her soon to be son-in-law, the wedding. It's important information you are gleaning, but at some point, you need to pivot.

➡ You + the pivot: ....
....
....
....

Yes! You must get the conversation back on track. Affirming their exciting news is a good way to move back to the point at hand, for example:

Things at our organization are also at a pretty exciting point—and that is why I wanted to get together with the both of you. I want to make sure you know the direction we are heading in, how your past support has already made a difference, and talk more in depth about your future involvement with us.

With all that is going on in Joe and Shirley's life, you might feel a little hesitant to talk about renewing and/or increasing support for your organization. It may seem that they are overwhelmed as it is and anything else will be too much. Yet, the fact that they agreed to the meeting tells you that want to be involved—and now is the time to start that process.

The fundraising process is often shown as a circle, or an infinity sign. That's because, while there are specific steps—Prospecting, Cultivation, Solicitation and Stewardship—the process isn't always linear and it is never-ending.

DONOR CULTIVATION CYCLE

As you know and we'll examine in later chapters, your best prospects are often your existing donors. So what looks on the cycle as stewardship may actually be cultivation for that next gift. And, throughout the process you should also solicit your prospects for numerous things such as names of other potential donors, introductions to prospects they know, information about people or organization.

At all points, your job as the fundraiser extraordinaire is to be moving your prospects and donors through the cycle, ensuing they don't fall off. The best way to do this, of course, is to get to know as much as you can about your prospects and donors.

Successful fundraising has been described as "The right person asking the right prospect for the right gift for the right project for the right amount at the right time in the right way." Finding out about all those "rights" is why we need to have compelling conversations with our prospects and donors.

WRAP UP

We've covered a lot of ground in this chapter—from mission to message, all tied together with values. Never again (we hope!) will you introduce your organization by reciting facts. Rather, you will talk about what your organization accomplishes and why that matters. Instead of learning an elevator pitch, you'll hone your skills in creating conversations— ones that invite the listener to participate with the goal of developing partnerships that will benefit your organization and the prospect.

Doing that means mastering the art of the pivot: Moving the conversation from the social to the specific and creating a space where you are learning about your prospective donor. It can also mean pivoting from what sounds like a rejection into a (compelling!) conversation that moves your prospect one step closer to becoming (again, perhaps) a joyful donor.

Values and the Case Statement

CHAPTER 2
ACQUIRING NEW DONORS

Each year, we spend $1 billion to capture, house—and euthanize—millions of dogs and cats. I am privileged to serve on the board of an organization that helps find forever homes for abandoned dogs and cats. On Sundays, from 2-4 we have open adoption hours. Could I entice you to visit us this coming Sunday?

Every day, children in our city come to school without having had breakfast. Often, these children haven't had dinner the night before. My organization provides these children with a free hot breakfast. This not only feeds their bodies but also helps to nourish their minds by making it possible for them to concentrate on their lessons. May I send you some information about the work we do?

All nonprofit organizations need a constant influx of new potential donors. If you are a school or a hospital, you have a leg up on most other nonprofits. These organizations have a continuous pool of new prospects—those who you have reason to believe will become donors.

For those organizations, there is also clarity about who will support you, and why they care about you. That clarity may not exist for your organization.

Nevertheless, identifying new prospects remains critical for all nonprofits.

The numbers on keeping donors in the nonprofit sector is dismal. More than 50 percent of all first time donors to an organization never, ever make a second gift. In addition, for every new dollar an organization raises, it loses another dollar (or more). These numbers are even more dismal for smaller organizations, according to the Fundraising Effectiveness Project (a project of the Association of Fundraising Professionals and the Center on Nonprofits and Philanthropy at the Urban Institute). The fact is that all nonprofits have difficulty in not just repeating their gifts but in making those gifts larger.

In this chapter, we talk about the conversations that can help to first qualify people as prospects and then turn those prospects into new donors.

THE WHY [OR MAKING AN IMPACT]

These conversations are as varied as the ways you would acquire new donors. All these conversations, however, need to start from the same point: What makes your organization worthy of support. That's not, as you might think, telling people all about the many wonderful programs at your organization. Wonderful they may be, but nothing glazes someone's eyes more than a recitation of "we do this and we do that."

Successful organizations tell you about the impact they have. In the opening gambits for conversation at the start of this chapter, we focused on impact and why your organization matters.

"The Why" is particularly important when you are introducing someone to your organization. Rather than saying you work with an organization that helps disadvantaged youth, grades 7-12, offering them tutoring, homework assistance, cultural trips to places like the museums, theater and musical concerts as well as matching them up with mentors—a statement that is sure to put anyone to sleep—utilize those values we discussed in Chapter 1.

Create a statement you might make in response to the question, "What do you do?" and compare your statement with ours.

➲ What do you do? . . . .
. . . .
. . . .
. . . .
. . . .
. . . .
. . . .
. . . .

Here's what we would say:

I am so lucky to work with a group that provides kids from poorer neighborhoods with the same advantages students in wealthier communities get. And it is amazing—kids in our program stay in school, stay out of trouble, get better grades, and more of them go to college. I'd love to share some of their stories with you.

Obviously, you'll want to tailor your statement to the situation and their interests. You'll note, that jargon or technical terms should not be part of the conversation.

At a workshop Janet was teaching, a director of development told the class that she worked for an organization that helps children with developmental and emotional disabilities through therapeutic equestrian activities—a comment that created a lot of blank looks around the room.

It turned out that the director got a lot of blank stares whenever she talked about her group. For starters, people didn't understand what "therapeutic equestrian activities" were and the more she would try to explain, the more confused—or distant—her listeners became.

Janet suggested she simplify her message and simply say that she works with an organization that uses horses to help children who have developmental disabilities (or simply "special needs") improve their abilities and skills.

Remember, you want to have a conversation—a compelling conversation—and that means you do not need to say it all up front. Your first objective is to pique the person's interest. If your conversation partner responds with "Horses? Wow. How does that work?" You are good. If she says, "Horses? I *love* horses!" You are also good. In fact, even if she hates horses, you now have the basis for a conversation. It's when she says, "Nice. It was good to meet you. Gotta go." that you have a problem.

PRACTICING IMPACT STATEMENTS

On the surface, creating an impact statement is easy. Simply state what you do—make it clear, understandable, important.

• You work for an organization that provides transitional housing for homeless families. Along with a place to stay, your organization also provides education and training for adults and day care for children aged 2-12.

This statement doesn't make your organization stand out, and it leads to the question, "Then what?"

➲ How might you introduce this organization to a new acquaintance?

. . . .
. . . .
. . . .

. . . .
. . . .
. . . .

Here's what we said:

Homelessness is a growing problem that actually affects all of us. No matter why someone is homeless, I feel a need to help, particularly when we are dealing with homeless families. So I love that my organization doesn't just offer food and shelter to these families, but also works with them to learn skills and habits that will keep them from homelessness in the future. And I know it works because over 60 percent of our families reach self-sufficiency within two years. Can we set a time so I could show you one of our facilities?

Before you plan how to introduce someone to your organization, there are a few questions to consider:

• Why does your organization do the work it does?

  • Is there a serious problem?

  • Can you either quantify or personalize that problem?

• What does your organization accomplish through its programs?

  • If homelessness, for example, is a growing problem, how are you helping your community to cope with that problem?

  • What changes because of what you do?

  • Who benefits?

• How does this relate to your values? Can you tie what is important to you to the work your organization does? For example, if your value is "equality," can you link it to supporting a living wage for everyone in your city?

Beyond values and impact, you must always have a call to action. Note that all our examples focus on getting the person to a next level; from hearing about the organization to agreeing to learn more about the work you do. Of course, not everyone will agree to your call to action, but they definitely will not move forward in their interest unless you invite them.

Focus on how you might engage a new prospective donor and write your own impact statement about your organization below.

❷ Impact statements:. . . . .
. . . .
. . . .
. . . .
. . . .
. . . .
. . . .

TAKING IT TO THE NEXT LEVEL

You met Susie at a chamber meeting. She expressed a real interest in your cause/your constituents but is not currently engaged with you. You call to follow up and to see if you can get together. Your goal is to move her from stated interest to involvement, with the hope that she will be a high level annual donor ($1,000 or more a year).

• What does the conversation to get the appointment look/sound like?

• How do you pivot from "great to see you again" to your purpose for your meeting?

➲ Pivoting from general interest to an appointment:................
....
....
....
....
....
....
....
....
....
....

Here's one approach to going from general interest to an appointment:

Hi Susie: It was so good to meet you at the chamber last Thursday. We talked a little bit about the organization I work for, and you indicated some interest. I would really like to share some more information with you and show you some of the work we are doing. Would you be available to meet for lunch next Thursday?

Note that we are explicitly clear from the get-go why we want this meeting. There is no room for a bait-and-switch (really loved meeting you and wonder if we could grab a bite of lunch and get to know each other better.) You *must* have clarity of purpose and share that clarity with the person with whom you want to get together for both practical and ethical reasons.

Besides, doing it this way makes that pivot easier when you are at lunch:

Thanks so much for meeting with me Susie. You seemed really interested in my organization at the chamber meeting. What was it that got you excited?

This pivot opens up an authentic conversation in which you can gain valuable information.

A COMPELLING CONVERSATION
TO SECURE A MEETING

At your friend Ben's birthday part, of all places, you met Matt and Jamie. As we tend to do, the conversation turned to your jobs. Matt mentioned that he sells office equipment and Jamie is an interior designer. After chatting for a few minutes about what they do, you tell them that you work at an organization that is committed to keeping young people who are living on the streets safe.

Jamie: *That must be heartbreaking.*

You: *Actually, it's often heartwarming. We see so many troubled youth—many just need a hand. Others, need much more. Could I entice you to come see our facility and learn about the work we do?*

Matt: *We would like to, but we're really busy right now.*

While you know that a tour is the best way to hook someone, it often takes months before you can get a prospect to agree to come to your neighborhood and see the work you do. Besides, at this point, Matt and Jamie aren't even prospects—at best they are suspects. But they are people you want to connect with.

You: I *understand, but I would love to share some of our stories with you. Could we meet for coffee next week?*

Matt demurs, but Jamie surprises you and says yes. You set the date and at the appointed time you meet her in a local coffee shop. You've brought your annual report and the latest newsletter with you. Inside the newsletter is an envelope—you are not hopeful, but then, you never know.

You: *I'm really glad you agreed to meet, Jamie.*

Jamie nods, but doesn't say anything. While it is tempting to jump right in and start talking about the work your wonderful organization does, you know that a much better way to engage anyone is by building a relationship, and that begins with a conversation.

You: *You said at Ben's that you are an interior designer. Do you work with individual clients?*

Jamie: *No. We are a commercial firm, mainly doing offices and, of course, lobbies and waiting rooms.*

You (laughing): *I wish we could hire an interior designer for our space! I mean, it's nice, but it is getting shabby and could really use a sprucing up. But then, we do get a lot of traffic.*

Jamie: *Do you actually bring the kids to your office?*

You: *Yes. We have an on-site drop-in center—and as you can imagine, in the winter especially, it's pretty packed. Plus, we have smaller rooms where they can meet with a counselor.*

Jamie: *And you try to get them to go home?*

You: *We try to find out why they have chosen to run away and be on the streets. Sometimes home would be worse. When that's the case, we try to find them housing and get them back into school or working. But for many, yes, we try to get them to contact their family and to go home.*

Jamie: *Are there many?*

You: *There are over 2,500 kids aged 12-18 on the streets today. We work to get them the support they need. We make sure they have food, safe places to relax, and other programs to help them get off drugs, out of prostitution, back on track. I really would love to show you and Matt what we do and see if there is something that resonates with one or both of you.*

Jamie: *I'll talk with Matt. Maybe we'll take you up on your offer of a tour.*

You give Jamie the annual report and the newsletter—and promise to call her in two weeks. You leave the meeting feeling that you have moved Jamie forward a bit and feeling that with their personal connection to your cause, over time you may have met two future donors at Ben's party.

THE BEST PROSPECTS

Meeting people cold—on your own, at a networking event or just when you are out and about—is definitely one way to try to build your donor base. But most of the time, the best prospects will be those brought to you by a board member, another donor, or someone on your staff.

Why are these folks the best prospects? It has to do with the definition of a prospect—which is an individual or organization that you have reason to believe has: 1) the ability to make a gift of a certain size; 2) an interest in your cause or organization, and 3) a connection to you. When someone who is already involved with you brings someone forward, you can assume that the traits of a prospect are there.

Sometimes, alas, although a board member says he or she has a "great prospect" turning that into a real introduction may be a problem. So an important conversation is the one you may need to have with your volunteers.

Before you talk with them, however, it is good to have a compelling conversation

SIX DEGREES

Board members often feel that they can't fundraise because they don't have anyone to ask. But we all have larger circles of influence than we realize. Looking beyond close friends and family can often lead to important doors being opened.

Brainstorm with board members about contacts:

• The people they do business with, both personally as well as professionally.

• Community leaders with whom they might have a shared connection.

• Friends of their friends and their family.

Bring a list of people you would like to approach—who do they know on that list? Who do they know who knows someone on that list?

The key is opening them up to possibilities, and to new potential donors they can in some way help you to approach.

with yourself. Be very clear about your role. Janet, for example, typically took on the responsibility of making the call to the prospect and setting up the meeting.

First, she would talk with the board member about the prospect and find out whether this should be a meal (breakfast, lunch or dinner) or a meeting at the prospect's office or home. Then she would ask her board member for three dates over the next two weeks when the volunteer is available. Finally, she would request the best contact information from the volunteer. In the example that follows, let's call this volunteer Casey.

Casey's prospect is Sam. Janet would call Sam and say, "Hi, Casey asked me to call you to set up a (meal, meeting) for the three of us. I'm Janet Levine from (organization)."

You can, on the other hand, ask your volunteers to make the appointments and work with them. You may need to contact your volunteers on a regular basis to ask if they have called to set up a meeting with their prospect. If the answer is often "no," ask what is getting in their way and try to be their cheerleader to push them onward.

Whether you or your volunteer (or you, if you are the volunteer) sets up the appointment, you should be clear about the purpose of the meeting.

- *Hi Sam, I'm calling to set up an appointment so we can discuss how to best get you involved with (organization).*

- *Casey thought you would be interested in what we are accomplishing. We want to meet with you to share that information with you and to talk about the charitable gift we hope you will consider.*

- *As you know, Sam, I'm really involved with (organization). Supporting the work we do is incredibly satisfying to me, and I'd like to meet so I can tell you more about what we do and how you could also become a supporter.*

You'll note, we are not being coy here. Rather, just as we were with Susie, we are direct about our purpose. Our first job, after all, is to qualify this prospect. If he or she is not interested in the work we do, would never support us, is too involved with other organizations, then few of us have the time to try to convert a non-believer.

Once you have the meeting, the real conversation begins.

LEARN ABOUT YOUR PROSPECTS

Your job is not to sell the organization or to pitch a project or program. At this meeting—and for many subsequent meetings—your first priority is to learn about the prospect.

You and Casey are meeting Sam at a restaurant of Sam's choice. Just as you would talk a bit differently with people of different cultures, gender as well as age should play a part in preparing for your conversation. Planning your conversation does not mean it will be inauthentic. In actuality, it will be more authentic when you prepare to do the best job that you can to represent your organization. Your prospect will also appreciate a well-planned meeting with a purpose. Also, the financial well-being of your nonprofit is too important to be left to chance. Before you head out for this meeting with Casey, consider these essential questions:

• What do we want to accomplish at this meeting?

• In order to do that, are there things about Sam we need to learn?

  • What are those things?

- What questions should we ask?

- Are there things we want to make sure Sam learns about our organization?

  - What are those things?

  - What materials should we bring?

  - What information should we have at our fingertips?

In addition, make sure you and Casey discuss who takes the lead and at what points. It's always good to have some cues—visual and vocal—that will let the other person know that either they should take over or, perhaps, they are heading in the wrong direction. Be sure to see our meeting planner guide in the Resources section.

Once you go through this exercise, you are ready for your meeting with Sam.

A COMPELLING CONVERSATION DURING A FIRST MEETING

You, Casey and Sam are meeting at Sam's office. It's the quintessential corner office, which lifts your spirits. On the walls are plaques from a variety of organizations, thanking Sam for his generosity and involvement.

On the one hand, this makes you feel great—the single best indicator that someone will support your organization is the fact that he or she supports other nonprofits. On the other hand, there are lot of plaques. You will have to work hard to make your organization stand out for Sam.

Casey leads off and thanks Sam for agreeing to the meeting. Sam flaps his hands and says, "I knew I'd get no peace until I said yes." However, he says this with a smile.

You: *Tell me, Sam, what do you know about our organization?*

Sam starts to talk, and you listen carefully. At one point, he says something that is not accurate and you (gently!) correct him, "Actually, we don't," you say. "What we do is…" and you go on to explain. Casey jumps in and tells Sam that, in fact, it is this very program that sold him on the organization.

When Sam finishes, you ask him about some of his other organizations—which ones are most important to him, what sorts of things they do that particularly impress him.

After about 30 minutes, you say, "I know you are really busy, Sam, and I want to be respectful of your time."

Sam: *I appreciate that and yes, I am busy.*

You: *So let me ask you this, how can we get you more involved with the work we do? Would you be amenable to another meeting where I can tell you more about our work and show you first hand the results of our efforts?*

Sam: *Yes. I would actually like that.*

You then pull out your calendar (or, if like us you keep that electronically, you pull it up on your phone) and see if you can make a second appointment with Sam.

After the meeting, make sure you (a) write up a call report, (b) debrief with Casey (How did Casey think the meeting went? What did he hear? What would he suggest take place at the next meeting with Sam?), and (c) send a thank-you email for the original meeting and include the date of the next meeting.

Note, prospects don't always follow our scripts, no matter how carefully we prepare them. Sam could have just as easily said that he knew little about your organization and cared less. He made the appointment because Casey asked him to, period. Or he could have started asking questions about how much of your income goes to programs and why are you doing this instead of that. However, that doesn't mean you shouldn't consider carefully what you want to say and always work toward moving the conversation in that direction.

WRAP UP

Acquiring new donors is an important activity for all nonprofits. But, of course, you can't just walk into the New Prospects Store and pick up a dozen. You have to compel these people to want to learn more about your organization and how they can be a part of what you do. The way you do that is through an Impact Statement. More than describing what your organization does, the Impact Statement focuses on the why—why the work is needed and why it is important.

Because what you do *is* important, it is critical that you understand how to qualify prospects and turn them into donors. The former is not about running a wealth screen and seeing if this person is wealthy. It is about having conversations to find out if his or her values and dreams can find a match within your organization.

Doing that means planning your interactions. To be successful you must know why you are having a meeting or conversation and what you hope to accomplish. This is true both for your initial conversations with your board members, working with them to open doors to their contacts, and through the meetings with those contacts.

CHAPTER 3
RENEWING DONORS

John, you and Mary have been such loyal donors to our organization. Over the past five years, because of you we have been able to continue serving our clients and increase the number of those we can help. I'm hoping that we can count on you again this year to make an annual gift of $2,000. It would mean so much to our clients.

Mr. and Mrs. Beezy, last year when you made your $250,000 commitment to our capital campaign, it really put the campaign on a different level. I know you still have two more years to pay off the pledge—but I did want to get together to tell you where we are today and how your commitment is making a difference.

Shelby, our President's Circle is our strongest giving club—thanks to ongoing members like you. We've been so lucky to be able to count on you not just to be a sustaining member of the President's Circle but to make your gift at the beginning of each year's campaign. Can we count on you again this year?

GAINS + LOSSES

The Fundraising Effectiveness Project (FEP) helps nonprofits measure and compare their annual growth in giving by gain/loss category and increase their net revenue by maximizing their gains and minimizing their losses. The 2014 survey report found these attrition statistics:

• For every 100 donors gained, 103 were lost.

• For every $100 gained, $95 was lost.

Visit afpfep.org for more.

We talked in Chapter 2 about the Fundraising Effectiveness Program (FEP). This is a project of the Association of Fundraising Professionals and the Center on Nonprofits and Philanthropy at the Urban Institute. Every year they publish a report on the state of fundraising in nonprofits across the US called the Fundraising Effectiveness Survey Report.

The report can be dismal reading. Pretty regularly, we see that donor retention is down and gains in new donors are offset by losses of donors through attrition. The FEP report also shows that the smaller your organization, the larger your attrition rates are likely to be.

That makes sense. Larger organizations have more resources to keep donors happy, such as more staff that have the ability to talk with donors about the impact of their gifts.

In this chapter, we will be looking at how your compelling conversations can help you to increase donor retention.

Speaking with donors about the difference they have made is critical if you want to keep them as donors. If the only time you start a conversation with your donors is when you ask them for money, they will begin to feel like an ATM and start to think that, yes, perhaps you are really just "hitting them up."

Thanking donors, not just at the time they've made a gift but months afterward can make a real difference in donor/organization relationships. So can conversations about the gift.

A COMPELLING AND THANKFUL CONVERSATION

At the end of last year, Keri and John responded to your end of the year appeal. It was the second year in a row that they have donated to your organization, and while the gift isn't large, it is slightly above the average for your donors. You thanked them for their gift within 48 hours of receiving it, and since then, they have received your annual report and your quarterly newsletter. It is now April and you are thinking that it would be a good time to reach out to them. You call and Keri answers.

You: *Keri, hi. This is Jean Kace. We've actually not met, and I am the (development/executive director) at Literacy Now and I wanted to call and introduce myself.*

Keri: *Nice to hear from you, Jean. Can I help you?*

You can hear hesitation in Keri's voice. She is, you think, assuming you are calling for another gift.

You: *Honestly, I just wanted to reach out, introduce myself and say thank you for the support you have given us. I don't know if you know this, but because of our donors, last year we were able to help 30 percent more adults learn to read than the year before. Your gift made a difference in our clients' lives.*

Keri: *That's so great to hear.* She laughs. *Sometimes you give a small gift and feel...I don't know, like it's gone into that black hole.*

You: *None of our gifts go to that hole! Every gift does help us to teach adults to read and write. And that helps them to get better jobs—or get jobs at all. Because of your support, Keri, our clients really do get a second chance to improve their lives.*

Keri: *I'm glad to hear that. It makes me feel so good about giving to Literacy Now.*

Just talking about the donor's last gift, of course, won't get you where you need to go. Your goal is to have a real conversation that will help you to better understand what motivates your donor, how they regard your organization, their hopes and dreams.

At this point, you see an opportunity to deepen ties with Keri and you begin to ask her open ended questions like:

- *I'm so happy you feel that way. Can you tell me what brought you to Literacy Now in the first place?*

- *Is Literacy Now an important part of your philanthropy?*

- *Who else do you support?*

- *What are the sorts of things that make you become a supporter?*

- *What do you hope for when you make a gift?*

THE MEETING PLANNER

While most fundraisers are pretty comfortable in social situations, having compelling conversations is about a lot more than a bubbly personality or an ability to string words together in a way that sounds good. Truly compelling conversations are the result of being intentional and having clarity about what you want to accomplish and the message you want the other person to receive.

Remember our discussion on planning your meeting in Chapter 2 and our introduction of the Meeting Planner? We use the Meeting Planner guide often. Consider the conversation below, and what you want to accomplish. Here's a hint: It shouldn't (always) be about getting another gift! Then refer to the Meeting Planner in the Resources section to plan this meeting to meet your goals.

LEARNING FROM DONORS

We are meeting with the Beezys who have recently made a large gift to our campaign. The purpose of this meeting is stewardship and we are hoping that we can get the Beezys' interest level up about things other than our capital campaign—and the fact that because of their gift, their name will adorn our new auditorium!

We will have to start where we are—and that means giving them information about the campaign (and yes, that auditorium). And, because we want to get them interested in other initiatives, we probably want to have information about these in our briefcase. But we don't want to "pitch" anything. These are there "in case."

What you really want to do is find out more about the Beezys. What else do they support? What matters to them?

You could just ask these questions, but consider instead asking them for advice. (Have you heard this saying? *If you want money, ask for advice. And if you want advice, well, ask for money.*)

Once you tell them about the status of the campaign and answer any questions they may have, you might say something like:

I'm wondering if I might pick your brains a bit? We want to make sure that our loyal donors really understand how important they are to us. Would you be willing to talk with me about what we do that makes you feel good about being a donor here—and share things that we could improve?

You might also ask them about other places where they donate—what do they do to acknowledge their donors and what do the Beezys think about those things?

To have a compelling conversation means that you must give your donors plenty of space to talk. So ask your question, and then listen. But listen actively. That means, above all, hear what they are saying and don't be thinking about your next sentence!

When Mr. Beezy tells you he really likes being invited to the President's party, don't just say, "ummm," but follow up. Ask him what is it about the President's party that he particularly appreciates. His answers will tell you a great deal.

Suppose, for example, he says, "I really like the food." That is such a perfect opportunity to find out what his favorite types of food are; how important good food is to his everyday life. If, on the other hand, he talks about the interesting people he meets at these parties, your job is to dig more deeply and find out what he means by "interesting" and what types of people he wants to have opportunities to meet. Just consider how much more meaningful a stewardship dinner would be if you served Mr. Beezy's favorite dish or had people he would consider interesting at the table.

◉ Planning your meeting

Think about an existing donor you want to steward. What is your first meeting going to be about? How will you introduce the conversation?

What things do I need to learn about this prospect? . . . .
. . . .
. . . .
. . . .
. . . .
. . . .
. . . .

What do I need to remember to impart? . . . .
. . . .
. . . .
. . . .
. . . .
. . . .
. . . .

The more you learn about your donors, the easier it is to engage them in meaningful ways. The more they feel that your organization adds real value to their lives, the more compelled they will be to support the work you do.

GETTING TO "YES" ON ANNUAL GIFT RENEWALS

Supporting your organization's work, of course, is what fundraising is all about. Along with stewarding your existing donors, at certain points you do need to request renewal of their annual gifts and to make additional major ones.

Annual gifts are those gifts that you can rely on year after year after year. They tend to be smaller, unrestricted, and support your organization's general operations.

Unfortunately, less than 25 percent of all first time donors to an organization ever make a second gift. Less than 40 percent of repeat donors renew their gift each year. How can you move those numbers upward?

In fundraising, the closer you can get to your donor, the more likely you are to get a yes. So, your annual appeal letter has several strikes against it:

1. It's a one-way appeal via letter or email and not a conversation at all.

2. It's an arm's length appeal, making it easier for donors to ignore.

3. The majority of lapsed donors are lost from the annual appeal when the letter is the only "personal" contact they may have with your organization. Too often, instead of a personalized letter, the organization sends a glossy brochure that doesn't even address the donor by name!

But your annual appeal letter can be a conversation starter. How do you make it more compelling for someone who reads your letter to say yes? It needs to be compelling—and compelling means personal.

"Our organization needs your help to do important things," is far less compelling than, "You can help us to make miracles. In fact, your gift last year did just that…"

Write directly to the donor, and that means knowing which donor(s) you are speaking to. A letter to a first-time prospect is different from one asking a donor who gave last year to give again this year. Reflect on your annual appeal and how would you start the conversation with an existing donor.

➲ Annual appeal—existing donor . . . .
. . . .
. . . .
. . . .
. . . .
. . . .
. . . .
. . . .

Because these are donors, your focus should not be on what you do, but how the donor's support makes a difference. Here's one approach:

Dear Sally and Bob:

Last year your generosity helped The Water Wheel provide clean drinking water to families in rural India. Because of you, Falik, her brothers and the entire village were assured they had clean, safe water. Illness, especially in children under 5, was curtailed. And we could do this only with your support.

MEETING IN PERSON
Now let's look at a donor who has made a larger annual gift. These are the donors whose annual gifts are of substantial enough size to warrant a personal visit. Your visit allows you to deepen the relationship with your donor.

After you thank the donor for their past gifts and tell them about the impact of their generosity, what might you say to help you learn more about this donor?

◐ 3 questions about your donor's interests.

1. . . . .
2. . . . .
3. . . . .

Like so much in life, what you might say will depend on what sorts of conversations you've had in the past. If, for example, this is a donor your organization knows quite well, you'll want to first review your notes of the last interactions with this donor (and here we are assuming that you write call reports—a sample of which is in the Resources section—and always look at donor records before you go out on a meeting). Let's assume that at that time, your donor mentioned that while most of his interest was in simply supporting your symphony, he did have some interest in learning more about the works you are commissioning.

John, while I know your commitment is mainly to ensure that our symphony has a robust season, you mentioned that you had some interest in the pieces we are commissioning. Have you heard much about the project we are pursuing with composer Sarah Kirkland Snider?

How might you open up the conversation with one of your regular donors? How would you go from "John, your past gifts have allowed us to..." to a broader conversation about what John wants to accomplish with her philanthropy and what her larger interests are?

◐ 3 questions about their philanthropy

1. . . . .
2. . . . .
3. . . . .

We are big fans of the open-ended question. You might a want to ask if there is anything specific your donor wants to learn more about.

John, your gift last year truly helped us to move our programs up a notch. We were able to serve more clients—and given our usual large waiting list—this was critical. I am wondering, which particular program of ours is of special interest to you?

If John tells you that he really doesn't know much about your specific programs—something that is not unusual for annual donors—we strongly urge you not to launch into a monologue about your various programs. Instead, ask some probing questions:

- *What first drew you to us?*

- *Of the things you do know about us, what most excites you?*

- *Would you like to come over next week and meet with the program officers and learn from them about their programs?*

Don't be disappointed if your donor came to you because of a friend and isn't particularly excited about the program that their original gift supported or your organization. Then, simply ask:

- *What can we do to help you feel confident that your generosity is doing what you want it to do?*

- *May I continue to communicate with you about your gift and how it's helped us?*

- *Are you interested in learning about our other programs?*

WHY DO THEY STAY?

Loyal donors are the most important element of successful fundraising. Dr. Adrian Sargeant, a recognized authority on philanthropy, has uncovered seven reasons why donors stay with a particular charity.

1. Your customer service is good.

2. They share your beliefs.

3. They're aware of the consequences of their generosity.

4. You've connected. And, you stay connected through multiple and meaningful contact opportunities.

5. They trust you. Your organization is effective and trustworthy.

6. Multiple engagements. You know how to engage your donors and how often.

7. They're learning.

Source: bloomerang.co

- *Is there anything else we can do to help you reconsider us in your giving plans?*

WRAP UP

Compelling donors to give, and give again, means having many conversations with them. Make sure that these are not all about asking them for support. Instead, tell them about the difference they have made and make it your business to find out more about them. Ask probing questions and really listen to their answers.

Whether your conversation is one way (as in an appeal letter) or far more personal, ensure you are having an appropriate conversation. Loyal donors don't need to hear how good your organization is—they already know that or they wouldn't keep supporting you. But they do need to know how they are having an impact.

CHAPTER 4
RE-ENGAGING DONORS

Good evening Mr. Sanchez. I'm a board member at the Fairfield Conservancy and I understand that until two years ago, you were a loyal donor of ours. I'm wondering if you would be willing the share with me why you no longer support us?

Hi Joe. I'm the development director at Housing Works. Two years ago, your generous support helped us to provide affordable housing for many in our community. You didn't support us last year, and—frankly—I'm calling to find out if there is anything we can do to get you back into our family.

Donor attrition is a big problem for many nonprofits. Many first-time donors never make a second gift to an organization. This is particularly true when the donor's first gift was given somewhat impersonally—as the result of an annual appeal, a special event, or some other arms length transaction. The reason is pretty obvious—the donor wasn't involved or invested in the organization and no one reached out to get them involved or invested.

The good news, however, is that on average, seven out of 10 lapsed donors will re-up with your organization if approached in a way that resonates with them. Usually, this means reaching out in a more personal manner. Most organizations, if they do anything special with their lapsed donors, simply send them a letter saying "We miss you," and hope for the best.

In 2007, when Janet started her consulting firm, she was concerned about her earning power. So when those end of the year letters arrived, she put them on a far corner of her desk and thought, "If anyone reaches out to me, I'll give them twice the amount I usually give to them."

After three years, not one of the organizations had even acknowledged that she was no longer supporting them. After five years, one group did send the "We miss you" letter, but when Janet did not respond, she simply ceased to hear from them.

Remember those statistics about donor attrition in the last chapter? Consider how much more solvent your organization could be if you could get even 10 percent of those donors back into the fold. In this chapter, we'll show you how.

KNOW THE ACRONYMS

When you work with donor databases, it helps to focus on donors who have given in the past. Two common groups to focus on in annual fund campaigns are represented by these acronyms:

LYBUNT stands for "Last Year But Unfortunately Not This (year)." These are your donors who made a contribution just last year and have not (yet) given in the current year.

SYBUNT stands for "Some Year But Unfortunately Not This (Year)." These are your donors who have given at some point, just not last year or in the current year.

YOUR LIST AND THE LETTER

The first step in getting these once-donors back is identifying who they are. If you have a donor tracking system, it is easy to run reports that will not only tell you who these former donors are but what their giving histories were. If you don't have a system, you'll have to do a lot of manual digging.

Re-Engaging Donors

We strongly suggest you start with donors who have given in the last year (also called LYBUNTs), working your way back through the years as you have time.

While we are not fans of the "We've missed you letter," sometimes the numbers make any other approach difficult. If you are going to send a letter, ask yourself what it is that might really matter to your donor. In other words we missed *you* because…

This past year was a great one for the Shelter—100 percent of our puppies and kittens found new homes because of the huge response to our fall Adopt-A-Pet program. We were missing only one thing: you. We hope you'll consider re-engaging with us and once again support the work we do. So we are asking for your help. Please tell us—what do we need to do to get you back?

Make sure your reply device—whether a card, email, online survey or your website's donate page for this appeal—has a place where lapsed donors can tell you what inspires them about your organization and what it would take for them to re-engage. You probably won't receive many responses to the question, but we feel confident that you will receive thoughtful replies from those that choose to respond.

Of course, a phone call is more effective than a letter, but caller ID has made it very easy for donors to decide not to answer the phone. (Still, voicemail is better than nothing.) Your opening would be similar to your appeal letter's opening paragraph. The difference is that after you ask how to get them back, your job is to be quiet and listen.

A COMPELLING TELEPHONE CONVERSATION

It's late afternoon and you decide to call a donor identified as a LYBUNT who made a very nice gift the year before last. To your surprise, the phone is answered after just two rings, and when you ask for the donor—Mrs. Carlisle—she says, "Speaking."

You: *Oh, I am so glad you answered the phone! This is Carla from Highland Hills. A few years ago, you gave a wonderful gift that helped our girls tremendously. We were able to provide special tutoring for our fifth-graders that helped get them ready for middle school.*

Mrs. Carlisle: *Well, that is lovely, dear. What is it that you want?*

You: *Mainly I wanted to thank you. But, I also wanted to ask you why you didn't respond to our appeal last year.*

Mrs. Carlisle: *Last year? I probably just put it on my desk and then forgot about it. I get so many appeals each year.*

You: *I can imagine. Our girls really rely on the generosity of our supporters to provide them with the resources that help them get a better footing in life. As you probably know, all of our residents have come to us because of a difficult home situation. We try to give them the support they need, but without our wonderful donors, we would, frankly, be shortchanging them.*

Mrs. Carlisle: *Yes, I was most impressed with the work you do when I first found out about you.*

You: *Then can I persuade you to once again become a donor to Highland Hills? You gave us $500 two years ago, and I'm hoping this year, you will increase that to $1,000.*

There is silence for a moment, then...

Mrs. Carlisle: *No, I don't think so.*

You scramble for something positive to say.

Mrs. Carlisle (with a slight giggle): *I'm going to contribute $2,000 so I can make up for missing last year.*

WHEN YOUR DONOR IS ANGRY

Alas, not all donors are Mrs. Carlisle. Sometimes they are not even close.

Indeed, lapsed donors are sometimes very angry donors, and you may have to hear some uncomfortable truths.

Worse, you may have to listen to untruths (or accusations against people who are no longer around) and your job is to deal with those unkind and unnecessary comments. How? By remembering the rules of dealing with difficult conversations:

1. Ensure that you heard what they said by restating what they told you: "I understand, Mr. Cagney. You are very annoyed that the last time you sent in a gift, you never got a thank you."

2. Don't argue. Look at it this way: You are educating, not debating. So don't say, "We do always send thank you letters," even if you do. Do say: "I can understand why you are upset. Your generosity is very important to us."

3. Note the importance of that word, "us." Always be on the same side as the donor. "I can't fix what happened in the past. But I can promise that I will do everything in my power to ensure this doesn't happen in the future. You are a valued member of our community, and we appreciate all that you have done."

4. Then, come back to the main point, which in this case, is getting this donor back: "So I do understand why you stopped supporting us. What can we do to bring you back into the fold?"

Not all donors, of course, are angry. Some stopped giving because they didn't feel invested; others had some financial troubles. Try to find out why they stopped giving and then see if you can get them back—now or sometime in the future.

> "I never learn anything talking. I only learn things when I ask questions."
> —Lou Holtz, inspirational football coach

I can understand how losing your job made you pull back on all your charitable gifts. So with your permission, I'd like to keep you connected with us, and when you can, hope that you will once again be a supporter. In the meantime, know how important you are to us.

Consider your lapsed donors. What might you say in a phone call to one of your LYBUNTs?

➲ Call prep for a recently lapsed donor:. . . . .
. . . .
. . . .
. . . .
. . . .
. . . .
. . . .
. . . .

Would you change your talking points to a SYBUNT? If yes, in what ways?

➲ Call prep for a long-lapsed donor:. . . . .
. . . .
. . . .
. . . .
. . . .
. . . .
. . . .

PERSONAL VISITS

Of course, good as a phone call is, it doesn't hold a candle to a personal visit (and yes, that often takes a call in order to set that visit up). To schedule the visit, think who on your board or among your volunteers might be the best door opener.

A door opener doesn't always have to make that call. Remember earlier we talked about simply using someone's name (with their permission!) to get the prospect's attention?

Making the appointment is a mini solicitation—your purpose is singular: Get a date on the calendar. So go in with some idea of when you want to meet and where. Then consider "The Why" from your lapsed donor's perspective.

Hi, Mrs. Smith. Stanley Grove asked me to arrange a meeting for the three of us. I'm the development director at the Mark Twain School, where you have been such a wonderful supporter in the past. Stan wants us to get together first so I can meet you and secondly so we can talk about the new ways in which the school is serving its young students. Would you have time next Thursday in the afternoon or the following Monday in the morning?

Once you get a meeting, it is time to plan your visit.

Carefully consider what you hope your outcome(s) to be. It may be to ask for a gift, but then again, if this is a long-time lapsed donor, it may just be that you want to reconnect and start the process of having the donor feel good about your organization once again.

Picture one of your lapsed larger donors. Jot down what you know about this donor—how long were they a contributor, at what levels, when did they stop giving? Do you know why they stopped donating? What else do you know about them?

➲ Donor history: . . . .
. . . .
. . . .
. . . .
. . . .
. . . .
Now, visualize what you would like to have occur at this meeting.

➲ Desired outcomes:. . . . .
. . . .
. . . .
. . . .
. . . .
. . . .
. . . .

Now let's consider the meeting itself. You'll probably start by thanking the donor for meeting with you and for all he, she, or they have done in the past. Then you want to segue into the purpose of this meeting. Of course, they'll know—you told them why you wanted to get together when you set up the appointment:

Thank you, Donna, not just for meeting with us today, but for all that you've done in the past for our organization. I don't have to tell you how much your generosity has meant over the years.

Now would be a good time to take a breath and see if Donna has anything to say. If she does, the rest of your rehearsed speech may have to be ignored, because it is critical that you listen and respond to the donor, letting them take the lead.

At this point, the conversation could go in many different directions. Donna could say nothing. So after a few beats, what might you say to Donna?

➲ Conversation starter: . . . .
. . . .
. . . .
. . . .
. . . .
. . . .

She might tell you to "think nothing of it, but know that I have moved on to another organization that gets my support."

Does this make you gulp and wonder why she accepted your invitation for a meeting? Are you ready to get up and leave?

Of course not! She said yes to your meeting for a reason, and it is your job to find out what that reason is and how you may renew Donna's connection to your organization. The big thing you want to know now is what organization and what are they doing that you are not doing? You might inquire: "I appreciate your honesty, Donna, though I confess that makes me sad. May I ask what organization?"

In most cases, your lapsed donor will tell you, and then you get to ask: "How did you get involved with them?"

Even if she won't tell you, it is fair to ask, "May I ask if there is something they do that we don't that made you change where you donate?"

Another possibility is that Donna says, "To tell you the truth, it never felt like my support mattered very much."

While your temptation might be to apologize profusely, the better way to handle statements of this sort is ask her, "Can you tell me more?"

You don't actually want to apologize until you know what you are apologizing for. What if—and this has happened—her unhappiness came about because she wanted a naming opportunity for a gift that was way below the value of that opportunity? You wouldn't want to apologize exactly, but rather explain about how your organization values naming opportunities and why she couldn't get what she wanted for the size of the gift she gave, important as that gift was.

At some point in your conversation, you need to ask if she will once again consider supporting you. Ninety-nine percent of all face-to-face requests should be specific.

Donna, I really appreciate your honesty and...

- *Again, I can only apologize for our poor communications in the past. It's not something I am proud of, but as I said, I can assure you that it is in the past. We've really improved our systems. So I hope you will give us a second chance and that we can again count on you for a gift of $2,500 for our annual fund.*

- *I am really happy that you still love us and not making a gift this year was just an oversight. Can we count on you to increase your gift to $3,000 this year?*

- *I'm so sorry that things have been a bit difficult for you this past year—but really happy that things are looking up. I'd like to invite you to be my guest at our performance next Friday, so you can see the wonderful things that we are doing. Will that work for you?*

Sometimes, asking why someone left or asking how to bring them back may not be the best way to re-engage. After all, you may know why they left, and not particularly want to revisit what occurred.

Similarly, if you know about a person's interests—either from conversations you've had or from call reports, you may have a perfect way to re-engage: "I'm so excited, Sally. You've frequently noted that we need to expand our services to the east side and we are finally in a position to consider that. I wonder if you would be willing to meet with me so I can tell you about our plans?"

Re-engaging lapsed donors is a critical part of creating a robust fund development program. While not every lapsed donor will return, you will find that the time spent re-engaging with past donors will more than pay for itself.

WRAP UP

Donor attrition takes a terrible toll on any nonprofit. Make sure you are doing all you can to re-engage your former donors.

LYBUNTS and SYBUNTS are those who once loved your organization's work and could love it again. Re-igniting their appreciation often takes difficult conversations; they may have ceased giving because of some real or perceived misstep on the part of your organization. Holding these difficult conversations is a lot like responding to objections during a solicitation meeting:

• Acknowledge what the donor says.

• Educate, don't debate.

• Keep on the same side; it's "us."

• Keep coming back to your main point.

This strategy works with any donor, of course, not just lapsed ones (come to think of it, it would work well with your spouse or partner, also!)

As noted before, planning your meeting is critical. Make sure you have clarity about the outcomes you are hoping for, and how you think you might be able to get there. Reality, of course, always trumps your script, but you will find it easier to deal with bumps if you considered the terrain beforehand.

CHAPTER 5
UPGRADING DONORS

Shelly and David—you have been such amazing supporters of our work. You have truly helped us to get where we are. And because of your strong support, I wanted to approach you first about making a lead gift to our capital campaign.

When we were at the gala, you told me how much you value our screen series. It is, as you noted, such an important part of our work. And for that reason, I wanted to begin exploring with you the possibility of an endowment gift that would ensure the series forever.

Over the past few months, we've been talking about your desire to make a truly transformative gift. We think we have a project that is just that— and for that reason, I've invited our program director to be at our lunch. Better than anyone, he can share the details of this exciting project and answer your questions.

Moving donors up is a critical activity for any fundraiser. Having a donor increase her annual donation from $100 to $250 and then $1,000 per year helps you to increase the operating budget of your organization, and begin to identify who might be a lead donor for your campaign or a large supporter for a specific project.

Typically, only three to five percent of your donors actually have the ability to make a major gift, though most of your donors could stretch to making a one-time gift that might be as much as 20 times their annual contribution. So, Barney who gives you $50 a year, might be willing to make an additional one-time contribution of up to $1,000 to support something that intrigues him. Most of the time, you'll be attempting to increase Barney's gift in more transactional ways, such as asking him to buy a table at your annual fundraising gala, or increasing his gift to the end of the year annual appeal.

However, if Barney were a $5,000 annual donor, there is every reason to think that he could make a one-time $100,000 gift—especially spread over a number of years. Giving at that level makes it well worth investing the time to learn more about Barney and sharing more details of your organization, perhaps over a period of months and several visits. In this chapter, we will be talking about how to do just that.

HELPING DONORS TO MAKE LARGER GIFTS

The first of these visits should lay out what it is you are hoping to move your donor toward—and get the donor's buy in. Notice the difference in the sample conversation starters at the top of this chapter. Yes, you start with the usual, but the tone is more confident—you know these donors.

You: *Hi, how are you? How was your African safari? I've always wanted to do one of those.*

Donor: *It was wonderful. We saw so many amazing animals. There was this one night when...*

So you let her talk, maybe show some pictures, but then you must pivot the conversation to the purpose of your meeting. This is not for the faint of heart. At an appropriate point (and depending on your donor, it may be when she takes a deep breath before setting off on yet another anecdote!), you need to say:

You: *That sounds awesome. I'd like to make that journey someday....but meanwhile, I do want to thank you for taking time to meet with me. As I mentioned, I want to talk with you about a very special project. Over the next two years, we are looking to double our capacity and provide transitional housing for over 200 homeless vets in our community.*

Now you have to do the hardest thing in the world: Be quiet. After a sometimes uncomfortable silence, your donor is bound to say something. Alas, it won't always be, "How wonderful. How much money do you need to get this off the ground?" She *could* say that. But don't count on it.

More likely, she will start asking questions, such as:

• *So how many vets do we currently have in transitional housing?*

• *How long do they stay?*

• *Do they end up in permanent places?*

Or she might say:

I am not thrilled with transitional housing. I mean, yes, they need a roof over their heads but, really, they need counseling more.

Or:

That sounds like a grand idea, but you know, we are really tapped out right now, and I doubt we could help.

Or:

I suppose we could move our annual gift.

ANNUAL GIFTS & MAJOR GIFTS

Annual gifts are given on a calendar basis and have a dollar amount determined by the donor. These are gifts that typically support your operation and which allow you to budget wisely and effectively.

Major gifts, on the other hand, are one-time gifts that are sometimes given over several years and typically are meant to support a specific program or project. These gifts allow you to build or enhance a project but do not figure in your annual budget.

When you are looking to move donors up, you may be looking to move them from annual to major gifts, or you may simply ask them to increase the amount they give annually.

This is the one thing you never, *ever* want your donor to do. Cannibalizing the money that supports your operations is something you cannot afford to do.

DEALING WITH "NO"

Let's look more closely at each of these types of responses and see how you can turn what feels like a "no" into a compelling conversation that may not result in an immediate gift but will allow you to continue the conversation over time. In our last chapter, we talked about conversations with lapsed donors who are unhappy or even angry with your organization. Let's revisit the first rule: restate what you heard. In this case, however, you may want to only restate part of what she said so you can add one of your project's benefits to better make your case:

You are so right—counseling is the key factor in helping our homeless vets. And we have discovered that the vets who are off the streets in safe and clean housing are three times as likely to go to and stay with counseling as those who are still on the streets. By helping us get them off the streets, you really are helping to get them into needed counseling.

While it is unlikely that this statement alone would provide your donor with a great epiphany, it should open a door—and you can then take your donor through that door by offering a tour, more information, meeting with perhaps a "graduate" of your program who has been successful or a counselor who can reinforce what you have said.

CONVERSATION PREP

Reflect on a special project on your organization's priority list for donations. What objections might a donor make?

➲ Likely donor objections to a gift request:. . . . .
. . . .
. . . .
. . . .
. . . .
. . . .
. . . .
. . . .

How might you turn that into a positive?

➲ Restate and redirect: . . . .
. . . .
. . . .
. . . .
. . . .
. . . .
. . . .
. . . .

If your donor pleads poverty or something akin to it, that's fine. You really didn't expect them to whip out a checkbook or credit card and hand you $100,000. Again, you restate, and move forward to the point you want them to consider:

I understand. You are so generous and we appreciate all that you have done. Let me ask you this, if you weren't tapped out—or if we were talking in a year or so—do you think that this is the type of project that would appeal to you to support?

Even if the answer is "no," you have gleaned very important information. Fundraising is all about building relationships and learning what motivates your donors. Almost as important as a positive response, is the information you can learn about your donor when they say:

- *Not right now.* It's up to you to learn when is the right time. In December? After they sell their beach house? In four years after their daughter finishes college?

- *Not for this project.* What type of project is more appealing to them? Is there any existing element of this project that might be interesting? For example, would they support the counseling sessions, instead of the capital to build the home?

- *Not at that amount.* If you've aimed too high, find out where they are most comfortable. Is the amount too high for their level of interest in the project? Or is it too much for them overall?

While "no" should always mean "no" in a dating or social situation, in fundraising it just means you have more work to do. Learning what's behind the "no" gives you more information to tailor a request that really appeals to your donor. It may also tell you that it's time to move on and you don't want to invest more time with this donor.

A (MAYBE NOT SO) COMPELLING CONVERSATION

Gavin has been a mid-sized donor of your community clinic for a number of years. For the past year, your organization has been in the quiet phase of a capital campaign. The public kick-off was a month ago and now you are meeting with Gavin to talk about a campaign gift.

Given what you know about Gavin and the fact that his annual giving has been in the

"I want to work for a company that contributes to and is part of a community. I want not just to invest in; I want to believe in."
—Anita Roddick, founder of The Body Shop and human rights and environmental activist

$5,000-$7,000 range, you are thinking of asking him for a $100,000 gift. You are not yet ready to make that request, however. This is an exploratory meeting where you want to assess his interest in the project and, if it is positive, what kind of recognition he'd be aiming for as a result of a gift. To make things smoother, you have invited Terry, a board member and friend of Gavin, to come with you. Terry has already made his commitment for a $150,000 gift.

After a few minutes of chit chat, you get right to the point.

You: *As I mentioned on the phone, Gavin, I wanted to meet to start the conversation about your gift to our capital campaign. For that reason, I asked Terry along.*

Terry: *And I was glad she did. I am really committed to this new building and have already made my gift. I think this will really be a game changer for our clinic.*

Gavin: *I don't see how. Spending $5 million on a building when you have so many patients who need your services seems wrong headed to me.*

Terry: *Let me show you.*

Terry takes out the architectural drawing, and starts explaining to Gavin what the various new spaces will be and, more importantly, how they improve the services the clinic will be able to offer the community.

Gavin: *OK, I see that. Sort of. But I still think that spending the money on bringing in more physicians and nurse and upgrading equipment would be a better use of these dollars.*

You: *You make a good point, Gavin. We do need more medical workers and we certainly could always use upgrades to our equipment. We currently do not have the space to expand. So by building this new clinic, we will be able to do the things you so rightly identified as important.*

Gavin: *So is any of the $5 million targeted for salaries or equipment?*

Terry: *For new equipment, yes. Salaries, no. We will still have to raise those through our annual fund. That's why we are asking our supporters to make an additional gift to the campaign—and continue with their annual giving.*

Gavin: *I really need to give this some thought.*

You: *Of course. What we wanted to do today is to let you know more about the campaign, and help you to begin thinking about the ways in which you might participate.*

Gavin, of course, isn't sold—yet. But the door has been opened. The next step must now be carefully thought out. Since Gavin mentioned equipment and staff, getting him together with the medical director may be a great next move. And, as they get ready to say goodbye, Terry suggests just that. Gavin agrees that he would be interested, and you now have your assignment: Set that meeting up.

But what if Gavin is displeased that your expectation is for a campaign gift in addition to his annual gift (an "Integrated Ask"; see Chapter 7), and says, "Stop! I've given enough." How would you make sure that you can continue the conversation, if not now, at a later time?

➲ Continuing the conversation: . . . .
. . . .
. . . .
. . . .
. . . .
. . . .
. . . .
. . . .

Let's look at one more scenario. You ask a donor for a major gift for some specific project or program and they want to support it by moving their annual gift to this new project. It is critical that you explain to them why that is a very bad idea for the organization.

We really appreciate your interest in this project, and we do hope that we can help you to figure out how you could fund this. What we don't want, however, is for you to use your annual gift. That support is vital to our well-being. As you know, the gifts we receive each year from our loyal donors like you, help to support our operation and is the foundation for all the work we do. We, frankly, count on your annual gift and budget it. Moving your generous gift to a specific program could hurt the organization as a whole.

Do you have another way to handle this (all too frequent) situation? If so, jot down some notes here:

◉ Responses to keep an annual gift annual: . . . .
. . . .
. . . .
. . . .
. . . .
. . . .
. . . .
. . . .

THE PYRAMID OF GIVING

Typically, when we talk about upgrading donors, we mean moving them up the proverbial fundraising pyramid.

You can also upgrade donors by moving them up within their tier. For example, a $100 annual donor might become one who gives $500 each year (or a $1,000 donor upgrades to make a yearly $5,000 unrestricted gift).

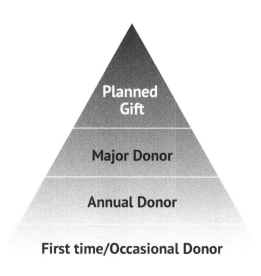

Planned Gift

Major Donor

Annual Donor

First time/Occasional Donor

Donors also move up and down the pyramid, so someone who is a regular annual donor, might make a large three-year gift (hopefully alongside his annual donation), and then go back to being only an annual donor, or may let you know that he has also remembered your organization you in his will or made another planned gift.

The important thing to remember is that fundraising is never static. It is ongoing—we should always be identifying, involving, soliciting and stewarding our donors in a never-ending cycle that engages and entices them to continue thinking of our organizations as something worthy of their support. That is why it's so important to sustain your compelling conversations and keep them fresh, strategic and authentic.

WRAP UP

Helping donors to increase their giving—by increasing the amount they have typically given, making an additional gift, or some combination of the two—is the holy grail of fundraising. Most likely, increased giving comes about because a donor feels a stronger connection to your organization, and that happens because the relationship between the donor and (representatives of) the organization have deepened.

Deepening a relationship relies on learning more about each other. Too often, fundraisers get hung up on "pitching" a need to a donor. Resist that. Learn how to turn your pitch into a conversation, listen carefully, and turn that "no" into a "yes" or at least a "sure, I'll listen."

CHAPTER 6
PLANNED GIFTS, ENDOWMENTS
AND BEQUESTS

Donor: *A gift of $100,000? I don't know what you are smoking, but I would sure like some of it.*

Development Officer: *I know that sounds like a lot, but let me ask you a question—if you could, would you?*

Donor: *If I could, I would give more than that. But I can't. I don't have that kind of cash.*

Development Officer: *Let's look beyond today—and consider the legacy you may want to leave the organization after you are gone. There are so many ways to make a truly significant gift that won't impact you today or hurt your loved ones tomorrow. Are you willing to talk more about this?*

Conversations about planned gifts can be stressful for both donors and fundraising professionals. With planning and practice, however, they needn't be. While some people feel uncomfortable talking about gifts that will be realized after their death, others recognize the power of leaving a legacy through a planned gift. As the adult child of a planned gift donor told Janet, "Reading my dad's will was so awesome. The gifts he left spotlighted his values. It makes me happy to know that his values will live on."

Making a planned gift is all about the donor's values. Although many gifts—particularly large ones—are thoughtful, planned gifts by their nature push donors to examine what they choose to leave behind and how they want to be remembered.

As you look out beyond the next few years, what sort of a legacy would you like to leave?

This question or one like it is what we often say to donors as we start the conversation about making a planned gift. Before you have that conversation, you need to have an understanding about gift planning and what it means.

Simply stated, a planned gift is any gift that is made as a result of the donor's overall estate plan. There are many books and courses that will teach you about the array of vehicles through which a planned gift is possible. These range from the most common type of planned gift—a simple bequest in the donor's will—to a complex Charitable Remainder Trust. Like current gifts, they can be comprised of cash, stock, personal property and real estate. Donors can also make your nonprofit a beneficiary of a retirement plan or life insurance policy.

Life Income Gifts allow a donor to leave assets to a nonprofit while providing an income for the donor or others for a period of time. Life Income Gifts include Charitable Gift Annuities, which provide the donor with a fixed income for life and Charitable Remainder Trusts, which offer variable annual payments for life or a term of years.

Often, when thinking about planned gifts, people get hung up on these vehicles and feel that they cannot approach someone unless and until they understand the ins and outs of each and every one of them. Nothing could be further from the truth. You will need experts who can help you navigate these waters when you get to them. But your job is much more basic. Your goal is to introduce the idea of a planned gift to your donor and communicate the benefits that come with creating a legacy gift at your organization.

The purpose of this chapter is to help you create the compelling conversations that will get someone to consider making a planned gift, and once made, will ensure that the donor continues to feel good about the gift.

BEHIND THE SCENES: BEQUESTS

First, let's cover some background about planned gifts.

For starters, most planned gifts are made as the result of a bequest. The Merriam-Webster dictionary defines a bequest as "the property or money that you promise in your will to give to another person or organization after you die." Approximately eight percent of all charitable gifts in the United States are made via a bequest, and importantly, more than 90 percent of all planned gifts are gifts via bequest. Most bequests are made not by major donors but, rather by those committed annual donors who care passionately about your organization.

For these reasons, we recommend that all organizations include two lines such as these in *every* fundraising appeal:

...... YES! I have remembered your organization in my will.

...... Send me information on leaving a legacy gift for your organization.

For many organizations, this is the framework of their planned giving program, and it is pretty much the only "conversation" they will ever have about a planned gift. But, as with every fundraising activity, the closer you get to a donor, the more likely that donor will be open to the conversation and will say "yes" and, critically, commit to a larger gift than they (and, perhaps, you!) first considered.

Asking for a bequest or any planned gift goes back to those values we talked about in Chapter 1. The most compelling request for a planned gift starts by showing how leaving a legacy in one's will (or via any other planned giving vehicle) is a reflection of the values the donor holds dear, and which the organization represents. Compare this:

Bill, by leaving $100,000 to our organization, you will ensure that we will be strong in the future, that we will be able to continue helping families in need and guarantee *that they have enough food and a roof over their heads.*

to:

Bill, we've talked in the past about how important it is to you to take care of others and help to meet their needs. This is one of the reasons you support our "Families First" program. Would you consider leaving a legacy of a $100,000 bequest to ensure that the help you provide these families will continue in perpetuity?

In many cases, you won't actually know your donor's values. In those cases, you can use your organization's values or the values that matter to you and are the reason(s) you work or volunteer at this organization. For example:

There are two things I love most about our organization: the fact that we treat our clients with the utmost respect and that we have a tradition of responsiveness to their needs. Because of these values—which I share—I have left a significant bequest to our organization. I wanted to get together with you today to talk about the bequest you might consider and the values you want to ensure for the future.

Beyond bequests, there are, many other planned giving vehicles—from trusts to annuities, gifts of real property, real estate and more. Within each of these there are variations to meet almost any need and desire. Becoming a planned giving officer takes training. For most of us, however, simply knowing that there are many ways someone can make a deferred gift from assets is all that matters.

Your job is to find out what your donor wants to accomplish with his or her planned gift—both for him/herself and loved ones, as well as for the organization, and then to ensure that the right advisors are in place to help. In the Resources section at the back of this book, you'll find a table that will tell you about the various types of planned gifts, and the value those gifts give to the donor, as well as a chart that outlines who are the best prospects for each type of gift.

MOVING FROM NOW TO THEN

How, then, do you pivot from a conversation about a current gift to a future one? Or, from a conversation about the organization in general to a specific request to be remembered in your donor's will?

Let's start with key questions. What do you think might be some details you must learn about your donor and their partner or spouse?

➲ Questions for a planned giving meeting: . . . .
. . . .
. . . .
. . . .
. . . .
. . . .
. . . .

Here are a few more questions to remember to ask:

- *As you look to the future of our organization, what are your most important goals and aspirations for what we could accomplish?*

- *Are there challenges we face that are of concern to you?*

- *What would you like to achieve with your generosity?*

- *What do you want to avoid?*

- *As you look out to the future, what is the legacy you would like to leave?*

- *What are your financial needs for the future? What are your concerns for your loved ones?*

- *What other organizations are included in your estate? How do you decide which organizations or causes to support?*

- *How might we involve your children (or grandchildren!) in our work?*

Discussing gifts that will be realized after the donor dies may seem like an uncomfortable conversation at first. With planning and practice, you will see that you are actually helping your donor to allocate their assets after their death in the manner that they wish, and even organize how they want to be remembered. So talking about planned gifts becomes a pro-active decision for your donors, one that will result in an important stream of revenue for your organization.

ENDOWMENTS

Although some planned gifts carry restrictions with them—a scholarship supporting a specific program to be used over a specific period of time—most are given without restrictions. Many nonprofits use these unbudgeted, and sometimes windfall gifts, to build their endowments.

Building an endowment is important for those organizations that intend to exist well into the future. We often think of endowments only in connection with large universities, hospitals and national organizations. But endowments are both worthwhile and possible for smaller, more local organizations. Indeed, size of your organization is not a defining factor. What matters is a real commitment by your board to the future sustainability of the organization and continuation of the work you do.

Endowments are pools of money that are invested. The organization can distribute some part of the interest earned each year. The principal remains untouched. Because endowment funds can ensure the future, as well as provide stability in uncertain economic times, talking about endowment can be a great way to segue into a planned gift. Endowment funds allow donors to create a long-term dream of what they hope to accomplish. They also demonstrate to donors that you are here for the long run.

A COMPELLING CONVERSATION
TO DISCUSS A PLANNED GIFT

Stacy and Ed are long time supporters of your organization. They give large gifts annually, and have contributed to some of your special initiatives. Your board recently charged the organization with building an endowment. Both cash as well as planned gifts are being sought. Stacy and Ed have been identified as possible lead givers.

Through a screening and rating process, it has been determined that they could make a gift of $250,000—especially if a planned gift is in play. You and your Endowment Chair are meeting with them to introduce the idea of endowment as well as the possibility of increasing their potential gift through a planned giving vehicle.

You: *Thank you so much, Stacy and Ed, for agreeing to meet with us. As I mentioned during our phone call, we are looking to build an endowment to ensure the future of our organization.*

Endowment Chair: *We're really excited about building up a fund, where the monies invested will remain invested forever, while the income earned from interest will be available on an annual basis to help us meet our mission. In fact, the board is so excited that every single member has made a significant commitment to the endowment fund. I, myself, have made a significant gift to this project.*

Ed: *I am glad that the organization is finally looking at an endowment. I know my university has had one for years, and it really makes a difference in ensuring that resources are always available.*

You: *Exactly. And that's what we are hoping for with our endowment. And given your past support of our organization, we are hoping that you two will become a lead endowment donor.*

Stacy: *We are pretty cash strapped right now.*

Endowment Chair: *I can certainly appreciate that. And, honestly, we are not asking you to make a commitment today. We simply want to begin exploring the possibilities with you. Would that be ok?*

Stacy nods.

Ed: *That would be great. As I mentioned, endowment is something we are both in favor of.*

Ed has just given you a tremendous gift—you don't have to sell them on endowment. You will need to move the conversation to options in which they can—in their cash-strapped moment—still be major contributors to the endowment fund.

You: *I can see that we don't have to sell you on supporting the endowment. But let me ask you this, if you were to make a significant commitment, is there a particular area you would want your gift to support?*

The conversation continues, with Ed and Stacy telling you and the Endowment Chair about their interests, hopes and desires for the organization in the future. Things are going really well, so you decide to take the plunge.

You: *Thank you so much for sharing your passion for the work we do. It is one of the things I love most about my job—I get to hear from our donors how important our organization is.*

Because you rehearsed these kinds of meeting with your Endowment Chair many times before this meeting, he knows that he now needs to step up to the plate.

Endowment Chair: *Ed, Stacy, like you I am passionate about our organization. So much so that as I mentioned I have made a significant endowment commitment. But, also like you, I was unable to give a cash gift of the size I wanted. So with the help of a my financial advisors, I have made a legacy gift. In my case, I have set up a charitable remainder trust that offers me income now and will provide the organization with a large gift after I no longer need the income.*

Ed: *That sounds interesting. Additional income is something we could use.*

The conversation could also have focused on the legacy that the Endowment Chair is leaving through his will, or the fact he has transferred ownership in his large whole life insurance to the organization; whatever planned gift he made would be the basis of the conversation. You would then move that conversation either to a direct ask or to an ask for an additional meeting with planned giving experts to help them make the right decision.

The first step is to have clarity about what endowment means for your organization. What might you use an endowment for? Note that some organizations have a number of endowment funds—some restricted and possibly named for the donor or person being remembered; others are more general. How do you think your organization would like their endowment fund(s) set up?

➲ An endowment is important to our organization because: . . . .
. . . .
. . . .
. . . .
. . . .
. . . .
. . . .
. . . .

Knowing why endowment is important is key to knowing how to introduce the topic to a prospect. Take a look at the following scenario and pretend you are Gina (or Gino!), the development director:

Hillcrest Senior Day Care is a safe place for older adults with cognitive or motor skills impairment. Their goal is to provide excellent care to all seniors who need their services regardless of financial ability. An endowment would help them to guarantee the future and be prepared for facility maintenance and other future expenses over time.

Susan's father was a resident at Hillcrest until he had a stroke and died. Hillcrest's development director, Gina, would like to approach Susan to make a significant gift to the endowment fund in memory of her dad. How would you begin that conversation?

➲ Endowment conversation starter: . . . .
. . . .
. . . .
. . . .
. . . .

. . . .
. . . .
. . . .

Compare your answer to our script.

Start by offering condolences and perhaps a personal remembrance, like, "Whenever I think about your father, Susan, I remember how much he loved our gardens." Leave space in the conversation to authentically share these memories.

When the moment is right, you might pivot the conversation and talk about the ways in which Hillcrest met her father's needs and made her father's life (and Susan's) better and safer during those difficult last years.

Gina: *We know how important it is for families to know their loved ones have a safe place and, frankly, that there is some respite for the caregivers.*

Susan: *Yes. It was important to know that dad was well taken care of and Richard and I could get on with the things we needed to do.*

Gina: *We're so glad we could be there for you, which is why I wanted to talk with you about our Endowment Fund. A gift in memory of your father would help to ensure that Hillcrest will be there for other families in need. We are hoping to raise $10 million in endowment over the next 5 years, and it would be wonderful if you would consider making a gift to help us get to that goal.*

Susan (an embarrassed laugh): *It depends on how much of a gift!*

Gina, wisely, stays quiet.

Susan: *I can see how important this is. But I'm not a wealthy person, and dad used up his nest egg in the last five years.*

Gina: *That's a problem for many of our clients—which is one reason having an endowment is so important. If we could keep our fees at a level that would be doable for our families, that would be so terrific. Susan, I know you are not ready to commit to a gift today—and, frankly, I'm not ready to ask you for one. What I do want to talk about is the level you think you might be willing to consider. Let me show you this...*

GIFT CHART STRATEGY

Gina shares a gift chart with Susan, showing how Hillcrest anticipates raising $2,000,000 over the next 18 months. Like all gift charts, it shows a few very large gifts at the top. As the dollar amount decreases, the number of donors needed increases.

Gina: *If you were to make a gift today, where would you see yourself on this chart?*

Susan looks at the chart. She is clearly uncomfortable.

HILLCREST PHASE I ENDOWMENT GOAL: $2 MILLION		
GIFT AMOUNT	NUMBER OF GIFTS	CUMULATIVE TOTAL
$300,000	1	$300,000
$150,000	2	$600,000
$80,000	4	$920,000
$40,000	8	$1,240,000
$20,000	16	$1,560,000
$10,000	24	$1,800,000
$5,000	40	$2,000,000

Gina: *Just to put your mind at ease—this commits you to nothing. I know that this is something you would have to talk with Richard about.*

Susan: *For sure. He would have a big say.*

Gina puts that in her notes—reminding herself to include Richard in future meetings with Susan.

Gina: *It's like that in my family, also. My husband and I make decisions about major gifts together. So, knowing Richard may not agree, at what range do you think you might consider an endowment gift?*

Whatever Susan says or points to, Gina knows that this is undoubtedly lower than what they will ultimately agree to. That's just human nature. And, of course, good fundraising. As skilled development staff know, getting a large gift takes a lot of cultivation and work. If you are willing to do that work, you are more likely to get a larger gift than the donor first considered.

Gina: *What I'd love to do, Susan, is to have you and Richard meet with me and our endowment chair, so he can tell you in more detail about our plans and the ways we hope to honor donors. Could we set up a tentative meeting now—pending Richard and the chair's availability?*

As you see, much of the conversation really is a way for Gina to find out necessary information. Gina asked a lot questions, responded to what Susan said, and didn't pitch anything. Nor should you.

Here's another scenario. You are meeting with a long-time donor. The purpose of the meeting is to ask him to consider leaving a planned gift for your endowment fund.

> "In the middle of every difficulty lies opportunity."
> —Albert Einstein

As you begin talking with him about a legacy gift, he puts his hands over his ears and says, "Don't talk about death. I hate that."

➲ This is a tough one, but we know you can make it work. Consider what you would say in response:. . . . .

. . . .

. . . .

. . . .

. . . .

. . . .

. . . .

. . . .

Now compare your comments with ours:

You: *What can I say? You are right. It's not a pleasant topic. But it's not death I want to talk about, rather the future of this organization and the work we do to make our clients' lives better. That, I know, is something that matters to you.*

Donor: *Yes. But yeech. It's depressing.*

You: *So here's an unpleasant truth: If you don't take care of how you want your estate to be distributed, the state will. And that's even more depressing. But let's not focus on that—let's concentrate on how you can make a real statement and help our organization best serve our clients. Can we talk about that?*

Donor (big sigh): *Yeah. I guess so.*

At this point, you would begin to use words you developed in your "case for giving" endowment gifts. But be careful—you want to be compelling not overwhelming. You should not spew out all the information you have, but rather keep probing about your donor's interests. And, unless you've recently had a conversation where he told you specifically what he cares about, don't assume you actually know.

WRAP UP

Planned Giving is an important part of fundraising for organizations of all sizes. While some planned gifts can be quite complex, many are very simple. Your job, however, is to start the conversation—not to hammer out the details of the planned gift—and then bring in whatever experts may be needed to finalize the deal.

Many planned gifts are used to increase an organization's endowment. This invested fund is an important way for an organization to ensure its future. Planned giving is often the ideal way to accomplish that.

CHAPTER 7
THE INTEGRATED ASK

Maggie, Ted. You've been great supporters of Food for All. Every year, you've donated to our annual fund and been sponsors of our gala. This year, I'm hoping we can depend on you again for both those things. And I want to talk with you about an additional gift—to help us buy a new refrigerator system.

Sal, I am so excited that you have agreed to support our endowment efforts by naming us as a beneficiary of your Charitable Remainder Trust. That helps to ensure our future. And I would like to take this opportunity to talk with you about our current needs.

Bruce, I would love to get together so we can talk about your annual Board commitment as well as other fundraising initiatives you may be interested in supporting this year.

The definition of the word "integrated" that we particularly like is, "with various parts or aspects linked or coordinated." This is the way we look at fundraising in general, and in speaking with major donors specifically.

Most of the time, when people talk about "integrated asks" they are referring to asking for annual or smaller gifts via multiple communication channels. For example, in the end of year appeal you would send out a direct mail piece, post the appeal letter on the website, put it on Facebook and other social media sites, send out e-solicitations, and follow up with a phone call. This is all great and good—and will increase your fundraising results. But these are methods for visibility on multiple platforms.

In this chapter we will share how you can use an integrated ask in conversations with your donors designed to result in gifts serving multiple purposes.

When you are asking a major or committed donor to make a gift to a specific campaign, you want to secure their annual gift while also asking for an additional gift. You don't want them to move their annual gift to the new campaign.

Imagine that Steve and Barbara always give you a $5,000 unrestricted gift every year. You don't want that gift to morph into a $25,000 gift, paid out over five years to the capital campaign. That serves you no good purpose. After all, the unrestricted gift could easily be used for capital, should you need it. But a gift for the capital campaign is restricted to that campaign (or specific purpose within that campaign).

What you want to do is ask Steve and Barbara for that $5,000 annual gift *and* another commitment of $5,000 additional per year for five years for the capital campaign. You might also want to ask them for a planned gift to help build the endowment.

Depending on your relationship and their inclination to make a major gift today, you might want to have to a meeting where you talk about their giving over the next five years. How would you do that?

➔ Questions to help connect donors' current giving to additional gifts:

. . . .
. . . .
. . . .
. . . .
. . . .
. . . .

A COMPELLING AND TACTFUL CONVERSATION: THE INTEGRATED ASK

Compare your questions to our conversation between the Development Director and a donor.

Development Director: *Thanks so much, Steve and Barbara, for agreeing to this meeting.*

Barbara: *Well, you know, we do love the work you do.* (Of course! They are committed donors)

Development Director: *And you show that each and every year with your wonderful annual gift.*

You pause a beat, to let either of them say something if they wish. This can get hairy. They may say something that could take you off track, so make sure you are clear about where you need to go. For example:

Steve: *What you do is important to us. We were worried a few years ago when (founding Executive Director) Fred retired. But the board did a good job hiring Stacy. How is it working with her? Is she as a good a boss as Fred?*

Development Director: *I never did get to work with Fred, but Stacy is amazing. I'm lucky to be surrounded by so many talented people—Stacy, and you two. In fact, it's your generous support I want to talk about now. Every year for the past eight years, you have made significant annual gifts. I cannot begin to tell you how important that is. That support allows us to do the work you so value.*

Barbara: *We are happy to support your work. Whatever we can do...*

Development Director: *I'm so glad to hear you say that. There is something more I wanted to talk with you about. We are kicking off a very exciting capital campaign, and we want to make sure that you are a part of it. For that reason, we are asking you to consider making one of the lead gifts.*

Steve: *We've heard about the campaign, of course. And we agree that a new building is critical. We'd be happy to have you move our annual gift over to the campaign if that would help.*

And here you have it. Your worst nightmare. Because of course, you cannot simply move the annual gift over. It is needed where it has been—to fund your operations. So you must be very clear with Steve and Barbara and, in effect, first say no to their offer, before revisiting what you actually want them to do.

Development Director: *This is a little awkward. I appreciate the thought, but to be honest, we need for your annual gift to remain an annual gift. We count on your support each year and frankly, budget it so we can do the tremendous work that is so important to you.*

What I am asking is that in addition to your annual gift, you consider a second gift—this one for $25,000 to help with the capital campaign.

Barbara: *That's a lot of money.*

She looks over at Steve, who is staring down at the ground.

Development Director: *Yes it is. The capital gift, of course, could be made over a number of years.*

Now you have a really hard task. You must keep quiet. Let them reflect on this. Wait until one of them makes a concrete objection, asks a question or makes a definitive statement.

Let's look at another scenario altogether.

THE INTEGRATED GIVING PLAN

Your organization believes that unrestricted fundraising is the hardest fundraising to do and, therefore, in addition to an end of the year appeal, which is generic, you plan "mini-campaigns" each year to fund very specific initiatives. This year, for example, in addition to trying to raise $75,000 in annual funds, you are looking for $60,000 for some needed equipment, $10,000 for staff development, $75,000 for a renovation project. In addition, you have a special event where you are hoping to net $135,000 (If you are a larger or smaller organization, feel free to add or subtract zeros). Every year there are also some smaller fundraising efforts that help individual programs fill in some gaps in their funding.

Some of your donors have complained that they feel they are being "nickeled and dimed to death." All of your board members are worried that you are "going back to the well" too often. What to do?

Ahh, you already know the answer: The integrated ask.

One time during the year (and yes, at the beginning would be ideal, but you cannot do all your fundraising in one month!), sit down with your larger donors and have the conversation about their giving for the year.

Marybeth, last year you seemed a little upset that we came back to you several times to ask for your support of a variety of projects. I wanted to make sure that didn't happen this year. Could we meet for 40 minutes so I could go over our financial plans for the year and talk about one, integrated gift?

Last year, Sal, you were so generous in making a $7,500 gift that supported our annual fund, a table at the spring event and the planting project. I'm hoping we can do something similar this year.

Michael, because you are new to our organization, I'm hoping we can spend some time together so I can explain the various programs you could support, and how we can structure your annual giving to meet your specific needs.

In short, your integrated ask is really an integrated plan where you have considered how you can best engage the donor and help them to meet their philanthropic goals while helping your organization meet its mission.

> "Much speech is one thing; well-timed speech is another."
> —Sophocles, Greek playwright

Often, you have donors who have capacity and are engaged with you—to a point. In three years or three months, they may be interested in making a campaign gift, but you have lots of work to do before you go there.

As you are considering your plan of action, you will want to consider how to ask for an annual gift, which they always give, and begin the conversation about that additional campaign gift.

If they are not a loyal donor, your planning needs to consider which gift would be the initial approach. For example, would you start the cultivation with discussions of the capital project and move them toward a capital gift? Then, after the gift is secure, you might begin to talk about how wonderful their capital gift is and what impact it helps to make, and then tie it to the annual fund. Or would that second gift be one to your endowment?

To know which is a better approach means knowing your donor and having great and probing conversations.

Cyd, thanks for meeting. When we met at Alice's you noted that our work sounded like something you could support. I'm wondering if you would share with me your expectations for organizations in which you invest?

As she talks, try connecting her expectations with the various things you do.

You mentioned, Cyd, that you want to be able to see concretely what your support does. Perhaps I'm being too literal here, but would that mean that the capital project we are working on now might be of interest?

Clearly, in these scenarios you need to know your organization's needs inside and out. This is your "portfolio" and knowing what the priorities are will help you to match your donors to your programs. The integrated ask also requires knowledge of your donor and astute listening.

WHEN YOU MUST CHOOSE

Remember, Steve and Barbara from the beginning of this chapter? They finally told you that they wanted to think more about their gift. What you are asking them for is simply a much larger amount than they ever even considered. Yes, they know they could spread the campaign gift over a number of years, but then for a number of years they are giving your organization a large contribution.

This is the moment where you need to decide if you want to keep the annual and campaign asks integrated, or if this is a time when separating them will be in your organization's best interest.

I completely understand. This is a big consideration. Can we count on your $5,000 annual gift, and come back at a later time to talk about the campaign gift?

Or you could say:

I completely understand. What kind of information could I get for you that might help with your decision?

Integrating these two approaches may result in the best outcomes:

I completely understand. Take all the time you need to decide on the capital campaign. In the meantime, can we count on your ongoing annual support at the $5,000 level?

Once you get an okay to that, then say:

Fantastic. What do you say about my calling you in a week or so to see if there are specific questions or concerns about the campaign I can answer, or if there is more information you need?

WRAP UP

Linking and coordinating solicitations is a terrific way to get commitments from your larger donors. By combining requests to support different initiatives, you can ensure that the donor understands the need for the annual gift even as you are asking for an additional major contribution. It is a way to show the whole panoply of things for which you need support. Even if the answer is not the "yes" when you hoped for it, you have planted a seed that is bound to bear fruit in the future.

Integrated asks are also useful to circumvent some donors' belief that you are "always coming at them" with a request for a gift. Instead of asking for this, and then asking for that, you make one pitch that covers the gamut of what you hope they will support.

As with all things fundraising, integrated asks require planning, a thorough understanding of your prospect, conversation agility and finesse. Indeed, we think of this more as an integrated plan than a single ask.

CHAPTER 8
FOUNDATIONS AND CONVERSATIONS

Hi Bonnie. I'm Katrina, the development officer at the Boys and Girls Club. I am calling to introduce myself and also see if you have time for a question. Are you familiar with our work at the Boys and Girls Club? ....I was reviewing your foundation's guidelines, and feel like our work falls in-between two of your interest area programs. Can you help me to figure out which—if either—we are best suited for?

Sally, hi. It's Paula from Ryman Arts. I wanted to let you know that Sheila, our executive director, was just nominated for the national "Heroes for Youth" award.

John, this is Marge from Chicago Public Radio. I'm working on a proposal for the NEA's ArtWorks grants, and I have a question about completing the budget. Do you have a few minutes to review the indirect expenses section with me?.

Yes, you can have conversations with foundation program officers—well, at least most of them, especially if they work a large foundations or government grant offices. Some program officers, of course, are not accessible; they choose to reveal little and avoid your phone calls. Some just don't have the time. They may be in a one-person office, or have more than just grant-making responsibilities. We find these program officers to be in the minority. In this chapter, we share several approaches you can use to hold relevant and compelling conversations with foundation program officers—while not needlessly burning up their time.

First, without a doubt, you definitely want to build your connections to your program officers. Why? Here are three reasons:

1. When approaching a new foundation, you want to make sure that you are on the right track with your proposed project.

2. Your program officers are experts in your field. You can learn from them and ask their advice.

3. Your relationship with your program officer may determine how much they help you, for example, when it's time to ask for a grant renewal, or should you need to request an extension on a deadline. Also, at some point, the foundation may no longer be able to renew your grant, and you'll want to ask your program officer about other funders. It's easier to have these conversations with someone with whom you have a working relationship.

Your goal is to establish a comfort level so you can fearlessly call your program officers.

GETTING THE RELATIONSHIP STARTED

Approaching new foundations is a necessity. While it may feel like a cold call, most program officers will welcome the opportunity to learn about organizations that match and fulfill their foundation's mission. Your research on the foundation's initiatives and preparation to demonstrate mutual goals is essential to introducing yourself.

Typically, you have two choices. The first is a brief email that succinctly describes how your organizations align and requests a telephone conversation:

Dear Sue,

I am Judi from the Community Health Project which reaches some of St. Louis' most vulnerable populations through evidence-based public health interventions: a syringe exchange program, and the Overdose Outreach Project, which trains doctors, medical workers, and their communities in overdose prevention and response. I believe our work aligns with the goals of the Milford and Lee Bohm Charitable Foundation. Do you have time this week for a brief phone call to see if this is a real fit for you?

The second approach is to directly call and we suggest this if you can say that a board member, or another grantee, or person in your field recommended that you get in touch with the foundation.

Hello Sue. I'm Judi from the Community Health Project. I met one of your board members, Linda Green, at a recent event and she urged me to get in touch with you. Our work reaches some of St. Louis' most vulnerable populations through a syringe exchange program, and the overdose outreach project, which trains doctors, medical workers, and their communities in overdose prevention and response. It seems our work supports your HIV prevention program and I thought I'd call to see if it really is a good fit.

It is very important that you prepare all your questions in advance of your email or call. The program officer may write back and say, "This is a busy couple of weeks for me. I'll be happy to answer any questions by email." You will want to write back immediately while you have their attention. You already know that there is some overlap between the foundation's goals and your organization's mission, therefore your questions will zoom in on details, for example:

Your website's description states that you support HIV prevention. We have two programs at the moment—the syringe exchange and the overdose outreach project. Would you consider supporting our organization overall, funding both projects, or is one more likely to be funded than the other?

Your guidelines state that you support programs designed to help adults. We primarily serve young adults, ages 18-21. Is this age group within your definition?

Although I have researched your recent grants and see that the range is $25,000 - $50,000, I want to confirm that this the correct range this year and for first time grantees?

BE GENEROUS

One way to build your relationship with your program officers is to share news and information. A good place to start is with news about your organization. Perhaps your board completed their search and hired a new CEO. Pick up the phone and let your program officers know. Or, perhaps the situation is reversed. Your CEO was let go or is retiring. Definitely, call all of your program officers.

Another conversation topic that hits the sweet spot of your program officers is news of other new funders who have approved grants for your project.

Thank you, Sue for believing in us. You were the first foundation to support our senior living program. I'm calling to let you know that the CommunityWorks Foundation just approved a grant for us.

Your program officer is an expert and they may have earned a Ph.D. in their field. They will likely know a great deal about their foundation's area of focus, but just like the rest of us, they can't be expected to read everything. You can share interesting articles, news about your immediate community, or a review of a recent arts opening.

News about your field or community is great to send because it flags you as a resource, someone who is thinking about their interests too. When everyone is asking your program partner for money, you can be the generous partner offering information.

Report writing also presents another opportunity to reach out to your program officer. As a rule, we email or call program officers after we have mailed, emailed or uploaded reports and proposals. It is not uncommon for submissions to be misplaced or fail to arrive altogether. You might also ask your program officer if they need anything else.

Hi Sue. I'm calling to confirm that you received our proposal? You know I'm cautious about the online process...

Foundations' submission guidelines are often quite complete, but your program officers are left with the job of condensing all of the information you provided into something presentable for the foundation board meeting. If the application does not request an executive summary, you can offer to write one. Or, you may have additional materials, such as a graph, image or video that will help them to make your case, but the online form did not permit you to submit. When you call to confirm that they received your submission, you might say:

Hi Cheri. We have uploaded our grant application and I just want to confirm that you received it. Is there anything else that you need? The online submission form did not permit extras.

Or:

The application did not ask for an executive summary. If it would save you time, I could write it for you today.

ASKING FOR ADVICE

You will also want to have a conversation with your program officers when your grant is coming to a close and their guidelines prohibit a renewal. This is a primo time to ask for their advice:

Hi Marie. It's been terrific to partner with you on our syringe exchange program. You have a great view of so many organizations, I was hoping we might chat about what we might do better in the future?

Of course, you will want advice on other funders. Before you ask, be sure you have done your homework and know who you are planning to approach for new funding. You are asking your contact for the less obvious sources of funding. Your program officers are experts and they are connected. They may hear of a new initiative at another foundation, well before you do. Frame your question indicating that you are knowledgeable about the major funders for this area and in your community.

Hi Sue. We've been researching foundations in anticipation of the close of our grant with you. I have identified three that look promising—although none are quite the same fit as the Bohm Charitable Foundation. I remember that you are often in touch with your foundation peers. Do you have a few minutes to review them with me? I'd love your input.

Or:

…We are talking to the Anheuser-Busch Foundation and the Emerson Foundation for next year's funding. Are there other foundations that you think are appropriate that we may not have considered?

SILVER LININGS

When your proposal is declined, it's not the end of the conversation—but another beginning. Your organization and the foundation clearly have much in common, or you would not have bothered to write that 10-page proposal. In this situation, you can email the program officer and politely ask if they are available for a conversation about your proposal.

Dear Larry, I received your letter indicating that our proposal was not approved at this time. I understand that your foundation can not fund every proposal. Still, I would like to learn more about where our program matched your goals and where it fell short. And is there something we should present differently next time? Is a call this Thursday at 3 convenient for you?

In your call to the program officer, you may learn how to apply next time, or what was missing from the program.

A COMPELLING CONVERSATION: TURNING A DECLINE AROUND

Laurie learned of a decline on a big grant proposal right around Christmas. She set up a call with the program officer and learned something unusual.

The foundation thought the proposal was great, but the board realized in reading it that the students in this particular program were on a path to success. The foundation wanted to support students for whom the foundation could make a significant difference. Rather than accept the verdict, Laurie pivoted.

Program Officer: *We loved this proposal because it really got our trustees thinking during their review. They realized in reading it that while we had invited this proposal to support scholarships for your advanced students, what they really want to do is be a game-changer for students who might not otherwise make it.*

Laurie: *If I understand you, our proposal helped clarify the direction of giving for this initiative?*

Program Officer: *Yes. They want to make a difference for the students selected and they felt that the students in your program were so accomplished, they are already on the path to success. I'm so sorry.*

Laurie: *I understand their decision but might I ask if you think they would consider learning about our community school students who qualify for financial aid? We have many low-income students at the intermediate level in our community school who cannot afford all the classes that they need to excel, for example, private lessons.*

At the end of this exchange, the program officer agreed to review a new pitch. Also note that Laurie knew her organization's "portfolio," so although she was surprised by the reason for the decline, she could talk about another program within her organization that might appeal to that particular funder. The result was a new proposal and a three-year grant.

BOARD CONNECTIONS

If you are lucky enough to have a board filled with well-connected individuals, they can be great resources for your organization. They are likely to know other civic-minded citizens, philanthropists, and people with a passion for your program area. When you are thinking of approaching a new foundation or about to submit a proposal to a current foundation partner, this is a great time to print the list of its board members and leadership to share with your board. It is always a good idea to see if your board knows anyone on the foundation board or staff and to keep your board members in the loop.

Their connections can be invaluable sources of information about the foundation, changes that are underway and whether or not you should even bother applying, saving you hours of grantwriting. Perhaps your organization is a little under the radar. A board member's connection can get you the attention of the foundation.

STEWARDSHIP

The most natural way to meet with your program officers is to invite them to witness your work. Whether you are presenting a performance, a talk for the teen LGBT community, or a visiting personality from the media, include your funders.

Hi Jennifer. I know you are very interested in our efforts in Afghanistan. Two IRC aid workers who coordinated relief efforts after the recent earthquake will be speaking to our members in two weeks. I would like to invite you to be my guest so you can hear their first hand account of the situation there.

Your program officer may often decline, but your invitation will keep them up-to-date on your organization's activities—as will the brief email or a program you send to them after the event.

When funders do accept an invitation, it is an opportunity for you to share more about your work, and learn more about their work and life. As mentioned in our earlier chapters on individual donors, you want to listen and learn. *What else are they interested in? What are they reading? What sparks their interest or grabs their attention when they visit? Did they recognize and speak with one of your board members during the event?* It is also a good time to take the pulse of their organization. *Has anything changed? Are they maintaining the same initiatives in the year ahead?*

When one of Laurie's top foundation funders could not attend a final performance, she invited the program officer to visit during the week when the young musicians were still learning the program for the big night. He saw students and faculty working—not performing, not polished—and he was thrilled. Laurie spent time one-to-one with the program officer and experienced his reaction to the lessons.

He saw students receiving feedback from their teachers—positive and negative—and the care given to help each student succeed. Laurie also arranged for the program's director to speak with the program officer. This was stewardship meeting, so Laurie did not ask about funding. But, when he left, the program officer said, "This was great to see. Invite me again."

WRAP UP

Conversations with foundations are at their core very similar to those with individual donors. An authentic relationship with your foundation partners is possible by reaching out to your foundation officers, sharing information, knowing when to ask for advice and including them in your organization's work. They are more than the receiver of your written proposal but someone who is also committed to the same issues that you are.

RESOURCES

Index of Conversation Examples..106

Websites...107

Developing The Case Statement...108

Common Personal Values..110

Planned Giving Choices...111

Assessing Planned Giving Prospects..116

Meeting Planner...118

Contact Report...120

INDEX OF CONVERSATION EXAMPLES

Chapter 1
• A Values-Based Compelling Conversation, 10
• A Short But Compelling Conversation—With A Pivot, 15

Chapter 2
• A Compelling Conversation To Secure A Meeting, 28
• A Compelling Conversation During A First Meeting, 33

Chapter 3
• A Compelling and Thankful Conversation, 39

Chapter 4
• A Compelling Telephone Conversation, 51

Chapter 5
• A (Maybe Not So) Compelling Conversation, 66

Chapter 6
• A Compelling Conversation To Discuss A Planned Gift, 77

Chapter 7
• A Compelling and Tactful Conversation: The Integrated Ask, 89

Chapter 8
• A Compelling Conversation: Turning A Decline Around, 101

WEBSITES

Association of Fundraising Professionals (afpnet.org)
Resource for professional development in fundraising.

Fundraising Effectiveness Project (afpfep.org)
A project of the Association of Fundraising Professionals (AFP) and the Center on Nonprofits and Philanthropy at the Urban Institute. Conducts research on fundraising effectiveness to help nonprofit organizations increase their fundraising results at a faster pace.

Janet Levine Consulting (Janetlevineconsulting.com)
Janet Levine helps nonprofits grow their ability to raise funds, increase donor retention and expand prospect pools.

Foundation Directory Online (fconline.foundationcenter.org)
Industry standard grants database and 990 forms.

Grantwatch.com
Grants database.

Grants.gov
Essential resource to research, register and apply for government grants.

Partnership for Philanthropic Planning (pppnet.org)
A source for education, research and advocacy for professionals who have a role in designing and implementing donors' philanthropic plans.

21/64.net
Dedicated to next generation engagement, working on multigenerational issues with families, family foundations, and donor-advised fund holders during times of generational transition.

Lilly Family School of Philanthropy (philanthropy.iupui.edu)
Grants degrees in Philanthropy, and The Fund Raising School offers 15 courses, two certificates, and customized training designed to bolster fundraising efforts.

DEVELOPING THE CASE STATEMENT

A case statement serves to clearly and concisely explain to others:

- Who you are
- Why that matters
- What you need
- How you want to meet that need
- What you will achieve when that need is met.

Case statements can be as short as a page or over a hundred pages long. They can be simple text documents or glossy illustrated booklets. Whether used as a "leave behind" or mailed, your case statement connects you and your prospects.

Writing a case statement serves two purposes:

1. It helps you and your colleagues articulate your organization's vision and impact.
2. It clearly defines what you really are trying to accomplish.

Many organizations have a longer internal case statement as well as an external "case for giving" statement, but two are not always needed.

To develop your case statement, answer the following questions:

1. What is the history of your organization?

    a. How and why was it started?

    b. What is it that makes your organization special?

2. What are the challenges you are facing now? These can include generic challenges to your sector as well as those specific to your organization.

    a. What might be the impact(s) if these challenges are not met?

    b. How would the world (however you define your world) benefit if they are met?

3. Give a context of your organization now—who are you?

    a. What is your mission and your vision?

b. What is the organizational structure and philosophy?

c. Who do you serve?

d. Who are your faculty or program staff? Your administrators? Your leaders? Your supporters?

4. What particular successes do you want prospects to know about?

a. What are the things you will build on from those successes?

b. Tie the stated needs back to this so you build a connection and donors can see this the whole gestalt.

5. What are you asking for?

a. Why are you asking for money?

b. What is the cost of the project?

c. How will the money be spent?

d. What are the long term impacts?

e. How will their donation make a difference?

f. What is the contact information for people wanting to donate or to get more information?

6. How will you recognize and steward donors?

a, Does this project have naming opportunities?

b. Are there any perks to certain giving levels?

c. Are there special dates/events that are part of this ask?

COMMON PERSONAL VALUES

Accountability
Accuracy
Achievement
Adventurousness
Altruism
Ambition
Assertiveness
Balance
Being the best
Belonging
Boldness
Calmness
Carefulness
Challenge
Cheerfulness
Clear-mindedness
Commitment
Community
Compassion
Competitiveness
Consistency
Contentment
Continuous
Improvement
Contribution
Control
Cooperation
Correctness
Courtesy
Creativity
Curiosity
Decisiveness
Democraticness
Dependability
Determination
Devoutness
Diligence
Discipline

Discretion
Diversity
Dynamism
Economy
Effectiveness
Efficiency
Elegance
Empathy
Enjoyment
Enthusiasm
Equality
Excellence
Excitement
Expertise
Exploration
Expressiveness
Fairness
Faith
Family-
orientedness
Fidelity
Fitness
Fluency
Focus
Freedom
Fun
Generosity
Goodness
Grace
Growth
Happiness
Hard Work
Health
Helping Society
Holiness
Honesty
Honor
Humility

Independence
Ingenuity
Inner Harmony
Inquisitiveness
Insightfulness
Intelligence
Intellectual
Status
Intuition
Joy
Justice
Leadership
Legacy
Love
Loyalty
Making a
difference
Mastery
Merit
Obedience
Openness
Order
Originality
Patriotism
Perfection
Piety
Positivity
Practicality
Preparedness
Professionalism
Prudence
Quality-
orientation
Reliability
Resourcefulness
Restraint
Results-oriented
Rigor

Security
Self-actualization
Self-control
Selflessness
Self-reliance
Sensitivity
Serenity
Service
Shrewdness
Simplicity
Soundness
Speed
Spontaneity
Stability
Strategic
Strength
Structure
Success
Support
Teamwork
Temperance
Thankfulness
Thoroughness
Thoughtfulness
Timeliness
Tolerance
Traditionalism
Trustworthiness
Truth-seeking
Understanding
Uniqueness
Unity
Usefulness
Vision
Vitality

PLANNED GIVING CHOICES

SPECIFIC VEHICLE	WHAT IT LOOKS LIKE	BENEFIT TO DONOR
Cash	Cash or check	Immediate tax benefits: • Deduct up to 50 percent of annual adjusted gross income. • Carry over excess deductions for up to five years.
Appreciated securities	Stocks, bonds or mutual funds that have appreciated in value	Twice the tax savings: • Income deduction for fair market value if security held for more than one year. • Avoid capital gain tax on appreciation. If used to make a bequest or fund a charitable trust, gift annuity or other gift arrangement, donor may realize substantial estate and gift tax savings as well. In either case, donor claims a charitable gift deduction of up to 30 percent of annual adjusted gross income.

PLANNED GIVING CHOICES

SPECIFIC VEHICLE	WHAT IT LOOKS LIKE	BENEFIT TO DONOR
Bequest	After providing for family and friends, donors can make an outright, residual or contingent bequest. The donor will need to make an outright bequest, spelling out the assets or property they will be leaving.	• May lower estate taxes for heirs. • Flexibility in that the bequest will generally be revocable.
Life Insurance	1. Transfer ownership rights to your organization of a whole life policy that is no longer necessary. 2. Name your organization as a beneficiary of an existing policy. 3. Purchase a new whole or universal life policy with your organization as owner and/or beneficiary.	When your organization is both the owner and beneficiary: • An immediate charitable income tax deduction of the policy's fair market value (cash surrender value). • Reduction in the value of taxable estate. • Tax-deductibility of any premiums paid after the gift is made. When your organization is the beneficiary but not the owner: • Flexibility in that beneficiaries can be changed at any time. • A reduction by the amount of the death benefit to taxable estate.

PLANNED GIVING CHOICES

SPECIFIC VEHICLE	WHAT IT LOOKS LIKE	BENEFIT TO DONOR
Retirement Plans	Name your organization as a beneficiary of a retirement plan.	• Eliminate the potential double taxation of retirement savings if left to heirs rather than charity. • Continue to take regular lifetime withdrawals. • Maintain flexibility to change beneficiaries if family needs change during lifetime.
Charitable Trusts	Provide income for life or a fixed term, with the residual (what is left) going to benefit your organization. • Cash, securities, real property or other assets are transferred into a tax-exempt irrevocable trust. • Donor chooses a variable income for life or term of years. • When Trust terminates, the remaining assets are transferred to your organization.	• Immediate income tax deduction for the value of the gift (the amount given minus what the donor expects to receive as a return through interest payments) that can be spread over five years. • Property tax will not be included in estate for purposes of determining estate tax. • The ability to turn non-income producing property into cash without paying capital gains tax.

PLANNED GIVING CHOICES

SPECIFIC VEHICLE	WHAT IT LOOKS LIKE	BENEFIT TO DONOR
Charitable Lead Trust	Can be a way to transfer assets to children or grandchildren with a reduced tax liability. Your organization receives a fixed payment for a specified term. When that term ends, the assets of the trust are either returned to the donor or passed on to the beneficiaries.	• If the remaining principal is given to children or grandchildren, it is considered a taxable gift. However, the value of the gift is reduced by the value of the charitable interest, lowering tax liabilities. • May reduce income taxes by removing a portion of income generating assets to the trust. • Distributions to Your organization are made now, allowing donors to see the benefits of their gift.
Retained Life Estate	Donor deeds personal or vacation residence to your organization now, but retains the right to occupy for life and continue to pay real estate taxes, maintenance fees and insurance on the property.	• Donor qualifies for a sizable income tax deduction in the year the gift is made. The amount of the deduction is largely based on donor's age and the value of the property. • Can immediately deduct the amount of the gift, up to 30 percent of AGI and carry over any unused deduction for up to five additional years. • Not subject to capital gains tax. • Eliminates federal estate tax as long as the life estate was created for donor and/or spouse. • During donor's lifetime, property can be rented to provide an additional source of income, or give your organization the right to use the property which provides a tax deduction.

PLANNED GIVING CHOICES

SPECIFIC VEHICLE	WHAT IT LOOKS LIKE	BENEFIT TO DONOR
Charitable Gift Annuity (CGA)	Purchase a CGA from a licensed source for "the benefit of your organization" and receive a fixed amount each year for the rest of their life.	• Initial purchase is partially tax-deductible. • Charitable gift annuity payments are partially income-tax free throughout their estimated life expectance. • Payments are not affected by economy. • Can be for one or two people, so spouse or other loved one can also receive lifetime payments.
Charitable IRA distribution	If donor is age 70-1/2 or older, they may be eligible to transfer funds directly from their IRA to your organization,	• Excludes the amount of their gift from their taxable income.

ASSESSING PLANNED GIVING PROSPECTS

Use the following to match prospects to planned gift products.

Age of Donor	Wealth	Most Appropriate Planned Gift Vehicles
60+	High	• Charitable Lead Trust • Charitable Remainder Trust • Gift Annuity • Bequest • Current Appreciated Gift • Life Insurance (Existing) • Retained Life Estate
	Moderate	• Charitable Remainder Trust • Bequest • Gift Annuity • Current Appreciated Gift • Life Insurance (Existing)
	Low	• Bequest • Gift Annuity • Life Insurance (Existing)
40-60 years old	High	• Charitable Remainder Trust • Bequest • Current Appreciated Gift • Retained Life Estate
	Moderate	• Charitable Remainder Trust • Life Insurance (new or existing) • Current Appreciated Gift • Bequest
	Low	• Bequest • Life Insurance (new or existing)

ASSESSING PLANNED GIVING PROSPECTS

Use the following to match prospects to planned gift products.

Age of Donor	Wealth	Most Appropriate Planned Gift Vehicles
40 and Younger	High	• Current Appreciated Gift • Bequest • Charitable Remainder Trust
	Moderate	• Current Appreciated Gift • Life Insurance (new or existing) • Bequest
	Low	• Bequest • Life Insurance

MEETING PLANNER

Before we go to an important meeting with a donor, or have a substantive phone conversation, we think carefully at what we want to accomplish. This form helps to organize your thoughts before the interaction with the donor and helps you to be strategic during your meeting.

Meeting with: . . . .

Others attending:. . . . .
. . . .
. . . .

Purpose of the meeting:

☐ Initial meeting

☐ Cultivation

☐ Solicitation

☐ Stewardship

☐ Other (be specific) . . . .
. . . .
. . . .
. . . .

Hoped for outcomes:. . . . .
. . . .
. . . .
. . . .
. . . .

What is needed for the meeting?
(Things to bring, information to have on hand)

. . . .
. . . .
. . . .
. . . .
. . . .

What things do I need to learn about this prospect?

. . . .
. . . .
. . . .
. . . .
. . . .

What do I need to remember to impart?

. . . .
. . . .
. . . .
. . . .
. . . .
. . . .

CONTACT REPORT

Date this report was filed: . . . .

Prospect Name: . . . .

Contact information: . . . .
. . . .
Assuming this person is in your database, you only need enough on this report to identify the correct record.

Contact made by (include everyone involved):

Staff . . . .
. . . .
. . . .
. . . .

Volunteers . . . .
. . . .
. . . .
. . . .

Date of contact: . . . .

Mode of contact:
☐ Phone Call

☐ Letter

☐ Meeting

☐ Other (describe) . . . .
. . . .
. . . .
. . . .

What was the purpose of the contact?

☐ Informational: First meeting/qualifying prospect

☐ Cultivation: Have qualified/moving toward gift

☐ Solicitation: Meeting to ask for/negotiate about the gift

☐ Stewardship: Gift has been made/all steps to keep donor connected until you begin cultivation of this prospect for any follow-on gift

☐ Other: Describe. . . . .

Pertinent Information: Any *new* information gleaned as a result of this contact?

. . . .
. . . .
. . . .
. . . .
. . . .

What happened as a result of this call?

. . . .
. . . .
. . . .
. . . .
. . . .
. . . .

What are the next steps, who is responsible, and by when?

- . . . .
- . . . .
- . . . .
- . . . .
- . . . .
- . . . .

ABOUT THE AUTHORS

 **JANET LEVINE** has worked in the nonprofit and educational sectors since 1988, beginning her career at the University of Southern California. Prior to starting Janet Levine Consulting, she was VP of University Advancement at California State University, Dominguez Hills. Other positions included Dean for External Relations at Pasadena City College, Executive Director of the Foundation at El Camino College and development positions at the American Film Institute, the University of Oregon and the Reason Foundation.

In addition to consulting for a wide variety of nonprofit and educational clients, Levine teaches courses in nonprofit management, fundraising and grant development.

In her for-profit life, she was a magazine editor and writer, insurance broker, and owner of a graphic arts firm. She has an MBA from the Graziadio School of Business at Pepperdine University.

She can be reached through JanetLevineConsulting.com.

LAURIE A. SELIK is a nonprofit professional with experience providing strategic leadership, creating fundraising plans, writing award-winning grants, and developing authentic relationships with donors. She is currently implementing and directing institutional giving strategies at The Colburn School in Los Angeles.

Selik worked for ten years in public radio, reinvigorating foundation support for American Public Media's *Marketplace*, public radio's business program, and launched *Weekend America*, where she was managing producer. Selik continues to consult in public radio, and often lends her skills to nonprofit boards.

Selik holds a master of professional writing degree from the University of Southern California and a bachelor of arts degree in communications from Michigan State University.

She can be reached at Laurie@CompellingConversations.com.

ABOUT CHIMAYO PRESS

CHIMAYO PRESS is an independent publisher of niche books that create compelling conversations, deepen relationships, and celebrate the human spirit. Launched in 2005 with one English as a Second Language (ESL) title, Chimayo Press has since published more than dozen fiction and nonfiction titles. Authors include teachers, radio professionals, screenwriters, and now professional fundraisers. The first book, *Compelling Conversations: Questions and Quotations on Timeless Topics* by Eric H. Roth and Toni Aberson, became the foundation for a series of ESL and EFL (English as a foreign language) titles.

Chimayo Press is named for the founders' amazingly communicative, talented, and loving border collie. They met Chimayo (the dog) soon after a visit to Chimayo (the inspirational New Mexico town) on a cross-country trip.

Would you like to review this book? We'd love to receive your feedback and start another new conversation! Visit ChimayoPress.com to see our growing catalog of books and authors.

43921221R00077

Made in the USA
Middletown, DE
30 April 2019